Pleading, Cursing, Praising

Pleading, Cursing, Praising

Conversing with God through the Psalms

Irene Nowell, OSB

LITURGICAL PRESS

Collegeville, Minnesota

www.litpress.org

Library of Congress Cataloging-in-Publication Data

Nowell, Irene, 1940–
    Pleading, cursing, praising : conversing with god through the psalms/Irene Nowell.
        p.   cm.
    Includes bibliographical references.
    ISBN 978-0-8146-3517-9 — ISBN 978-0-8146-3542-1 (e-book)
    1. Bible. O.T. Psalms—Prayers.   I. Title.
    BS1430.55.N69   2013
    223'.206—dc23   2012042298

For Daniel Durken, OSB,
who first encouraged me
to write about the Psalms.

Contents

Preface

I have lived with the Psalms most of my life. My monastic community prays them daily, and throughout the course of four weeks we pray the entire Psalter. My educational journey has also taken me to the Psalms. My undergraduate degree is in music, but after college I took a detour to study languages, particularly German. Finally I found my true love: Scripture. That somewhat disorganized journey led me inevitably to the Psalms. Where else can you find a subject that includes singing, language, and Bible?

My aim in writing this book is to encourage you not only to use the Psalms as your prayerbook but also to use them as models for additional personal prayer. I am convinced that the Psalms teach us to pray. I suggest that, as you read this book, you keep a Psalm book handy to ponder other psalms that teach us to tell our story, cry out our pain, and give praise to God. (At the end of the book is a table listing laments, thanksgiving psalms, hymns, etc.) In addition, I encourage you to write your own psalm-prayers. I have added exercises to the end of several chapters as an aid for this endeavor.

As you read this book, you will see signs of its long gestation. It originated with a few talks given to the chapter of the Federation of St. Scholastica. The talks then grew into a retreat that I enjoyed sharing with many communities across the country. Along the way some of the material also appeared in print. Now I am responding gratefully to the suggestion of Father Daniel Durken, OSB, to turn the spoken word into the book that you have in your hands.

It is impossible for me to list all the people to whom I am grateful for having shaped the material in this book. I thank Abbot Gregory Polan, OSB, of Conception Abbey, my lifelong friend, for his excellent translation of the Psalms in the *Revised Grail Psalter*. He is a worthy follower of his insightful patron, Gregory the Great. I thank Michael Boschert at GIA for permission to quote Abbot Gregory's translation. I am grateful to Father Michael Casey, OCSO, for permission to print material from my article that appeared in *Tjurunga*. To all my friends at Liturgical Press, too many to be named, I say, "Thank you!" Your encouragement has been a great gift to me. Finally, I am deeply grateful to my wonderful community at Mount St. Scholastica. What I know about praying the Psalms I learned from my sisters.

Irene Nowell, OSB

Begin at the Beginning:
"If you would be happy" (Ps 1)

When I was a sophomore in high school, my English teacher used to quote the psalms to us all the time. She frequently said, "It's so good to be a Benedictine. The psalms just soak into your bones." I entered monastic life for a lot of the wrong reasons— or reasons I did not know—but one of the right reasons was because I wanted the psalms to "soak into my bones." Gradually I came to realize that, even here, Sister Lillian Muell was quoting the psalms. Psalm 1 tells us that if we ponder the law of the Lord day and night, we will be like trees planted by a flowing stream. The Psalter (the book of Psalms) is a distillation of God's law. So the law of the Lord, the Word of God in the psalms we pray day by day, will soak into our bones, refreshing and nourishing us, giving us life.[1]

What does it mean that the psalms will soak into our bones? What kind of people will we become if we pray the psalms regularly, daily? Demetrius Dumm uses the image of a Crock-Pot, which tenderizes even the toughest cuts of meat.

He observes that "many a tough-willed monastic has been made docile and gentle before God by faithful praying of the psalms."[2] Allan Bouley, OSB, suggests another image: The psalms are like a marinade that both tenderizes and adds flavor to our lives. Perhaps you have another image. Regardless, it is the questions that are significant: What kind of people will we become if we pray the psalms? What do the psalms teach us about how to live well? What is the effect on us of praying and pondering them regularly? Several years ago Pope John Paul II said in one of his Wednesday audiences, "the Book of Psalms remains the ideal source of Christian prayer, and will continue to inspire the Church in the new millennium."[3] The psalms are a gift for all of us, whether we are professed religious or faithful laypeople.

The introduction to any book tells us many things: the purpose of the author, the author's style, the basic content, and, perhaps, the organization of the book. So what is the introduction to the Psalter? Let us use our skills in *lectio divina* (slow, thoughtful reading) to ponder Psalm 1. What can this introductory psalm tell us about why we pray the Psalms and what their effect on us will be?

We begin with happiness. The first word of the Psalter is "happy," in Hebrew, *'ashre*. From its first word this little book of 150 song-prayers promises to tell us how to be happy—truly, deeply happy. But the psalm does not begin with a recipe for happiness. Rather it begins by telling us what to avoid: "never walk with the wicked, / never stand with sinners, / never sit among cynics."[4] This psalm shows us that happiness is clearly a communal virtue! If we associate with the wicked, sinners, and cynics, we will become like them. The first verse of the Psalter implies that these people are not happy!

Who are these people we are advised to avoid? The first two terms—wicked and sinners—are generic. But the third term—in Hebrew, *letsim*, meaning "cynics" or "scoffers"—is more specific. The people we are warned to avoid if we want to be happy are not named as murderers or adulterers, embezzlers or muggers. They are the naysayers among us. These are people like Job's friends who scorn him and attempt to convince him that he is a sinner (see Job 16:20). According to Proverbs, they are proud and haughty and act with arrogance (Prov 21:24). These people have closed all the doors and are unable to be open to anything new that God might have to offer. Do you know any of these people? Have you ever met someone who always knows better than those in authority? Or who is wiser than the wisdom of the whole group and lies in wait for a community or family decision to fail? Saint Benedict calls these people "murmurers" or "grumblers," and he is insistent that this danger be rooted out; "Above all else we admonish them to refrain from grumbling" (RB 40.9).[5]

The progression of verbs in these first verses of Psalm 1 is also significant: walk, stand, sit. Psalm 1, the introduction to the Psalter, warns us that if we would be happy we should avoid getting drawn into a murmuring session: first strolling along, then standing in doorways or on street corners, and finally sitting down with a cup of coffee, grousing away. If you would be happy, don't do this!

So what *should* we do? Psalm 1 goes on to tell us that a person who is happy is one "whose delight is the law [Hebrew, *torah*] of the LORD, and who ponders his law day and night" (Ps 1:2).[6] Where and how does God teach us? When we think of *torah*, we think first of the Bible and especially the first five books, the Pentateuch. Scripture is God's word to us, God's teaching. It is the way God speaks to us day after day. Second, Psalm 1 may be referring in a special way to the Psalter itself as God's *torah*. Some ancient editor divided the Psalter into five books in imitation of the Pentateuch. Look at the final verses of Psalms 41, 72, 89, and 106. Each one ends by saying, "Blest be the LORD," and, "Amen." Psalm 106 adds, "Alleluia!" These closings are similar to the practice of adding the doxology, "Glory to the Father," to the end of a psalm. They indicate that a section is finished. This ancient editor wanted to tell us that the Psalter was a mini-Pentateuch, God's law in a pocket version, so we can delight in and ponder it night and day.

Finally, God's *torah* is written for us in the people with whom we live and work and in all the wonders of creation and culture. We find God's *torah* in a beautiful sunset, in a Mozart symphony, in a child's first word. In his Letter to the Philippians, St. Paul gives us this advice: "whatever is true, whatever is honorable, whatever is just, whatever is pure, whatever is pleasing, whatever is commendable, if there is any excellence and if there is anything worthy of praise, think about these things" (Phil 4:8).[7] God's teaching comes to us in all these ways. If God's teaching fills our thoughts and delights our hearts, then we will be truly happy.

Delighting in our hearts, however, is not enough. Verse 2 of Psalm 1 tells us not only to delight but also to "ponder," "meditate," and "study" God's *torah*. The Hebrew word, *yehgeh*, literally means to "mutter" or to "growl." The idea is related to the tradition of vocal prayer and also to the fact that in the ancient world almost no one read silently. So those praying or meditating "muttered" or "murmured." You may have seen Jews at the Western Wall or Muslims in a mosque murmuring their prayers. You may also have heard someone whispering the rosary as she prayed. Bruno Barnhart, OSB-Cam, recommends this "murmuring" for anyone practicing *lectio divina*: Memorize a verse and carry it around like the desert monks; murmur it so you have a "muscular memory" of it.[8] Paradoxically, Psalm 1 tells us to avoid murmurers and that murmuring will make us happy—but only if what we are murmuring is God's *torah*, God's word to us.

To summarize, the first two verses of the Psalter promise us that, if we want to be happy, we must avoid the wicked and cynical murmurers and rejoice in God's teaching, murmuring the Word night and day (see Ps 1:1-2).

What else happens to us as we pray the psalms? We began with happiness. What other insights are here for us? First of all, praying the psalms will lead us to become people who listen. This is the first injunction of Saint Benedict to his followers: "Listen with the ear of your heart" (RB Prol 1). It is also the beginning of the Jewish daily prayer, the *Shema*: "Hear, O Israel: The Lord is our God, the Lord alone. You shall love the Lord your God with all your heart, and with all your soul, and with all your might" (Deut 6:4-5). The psalms demand of us careful attention. The listening they require must be constant and tuned to many voices: the voice of God, the voice of Christ, and the voices of all humankind. Saint Benedict also names the daily communal praying of the psalms the *Opus Dei*, "Work of God." The listening demanded by the psalms is, indeed, hard work!

The first voice that we hear in the psalms is the voice of God. The psalms that we pray day after day are a part of Scripture—that privileged text that we honor as the Word of God. So we come to them daily with the same question: What is it that God wants to say to me today through these words? We have a right and a duty to expect to hear the voice of God in the psalms—every day. Every day that word will be different: sometimes challenging and sometimes comforting, sometimes the still, small sound of silence and sometimes the roar of the devouring fire. Every day as we listen to the words of the psalms we listen to the voice of God.

I suspect, however, that most people who pray the psalms do not often reflect on this truth. We can become so focused on our own voices in the psalms, our own prayer, that we forget that the first voice we hear is the voice of God. That inattention can be dangerous. We may miss this all-important word addressed to us. It is guaranteed that today, as we pray the psalms, we will hear the voice of God (see Ps 95:7). What is not guaranteed is that we will be listening!

The second voice that we Christians hear in the psalms, if we are listening, is the voice of Christ. We must not forget that the psalms are the prayerbook of Jesus. When we pray them, we join our voices to his. The early Christian writers were aware of the presence of Christ in the Psalms. Saint Augustine's massive work, *Expositions on the Psalms,*[9] is a clear example of this, as are works of Saints Ambrose and Jerome and others. In one of his Wednesday audiences in 2001, Pope John Paul II said that these early Christian writers "were able with deep spiritual penetration to discern and identify the great 'key' to understanding the Psalms as Christ himself. . . . Christians were thus able to read the Book of Psalms in the light of the whole mystery of Christ."[10]

Saint Augustine, in particular, emphasizes the presence of Christ in the psalms, not only as head, but also in all the members of his body, especially the poor and suffering. This brings us to the third voice we hear in the psalms: the human voice, the voices of Christ's members. We hear our own voices; we hear the voices of our brothers and sisters who are praying with us. We hear the voices crying out throughout the world. We realize how very human these prayers are.

There are serious implications that flow from listening to and praying with the human voices in the psalms. The first human voice my ears hear as I pray is my own. Do I believe that it is possible for me to speak with the voice of God? If I speak the Word of God in prayer, how careful must I be with my words in other situations? Second, if we are fortunate enough to be praying the psalms in a group, we hear the voices of those who are praying with us. What does this teach me about listening to those voices in other situations? Finally, we hear the voices of all humankind, especially those most in need. What can I do to be more attuned to these other voices: the poor, the refugees, the immigrants, the victimized, the trafficked, the sick, the imprisoned? A useful exercise for *lectio divina* is to take the psalm book in one hand and the daily newspaper in the other. After every few psalm verses, read another headline. The voices that cry out in the daily news also cry out in the psalm. Every time we pray the psalms we pray in the name of the whole body of Christ, in the name of the whole world. We carry all those people in our prayer; by praying the psalms we take responsibility for the well-being of all of them.

The illuminations in the book of Psalms of *The Saint John's Bible* are a dramatic reminder of our oneness with all people as we pray the psalms.[11] Running horizontally across the page are voice prints, oscilloscopes, of the Saint John's monks praying the psalms. This is not a dead letter; it is a living word. But running vertically across the illuminations are other voice prints from other traditions: Jewish, Native American, Greek Orthodox, Buddhist, Taoist, Muslim. The faithful in all these traditions sing praise to God. When we sing the Psalms, we join our voices with theirs.

Susannah Heschel, daughter of the great Jewish theologian Abraham Joshua Heschel, said this about her father: "Religion evokes obligation and the certainty that something is asked of us, that there are ends which are in need of us. God, he once wrote, 'is not only a power we depend on; He is a God who demands. God poses a challenge to go beyond ourselves—and it is precisely that going beyond, that awareness of challenge, that constitutes our being. We often forget this, so prayer comes as a reminder that over and above personal problems, there is an objective challenge to overcome inequity, helplessness, suffering, carelessness, and oppression.' "[12] We acknowledge that "objective challenge" as we pray the psalms.

Again, praying the Psalms leads us to become people who listen—who listen to the voice of God, the voice of Christ, our own voice, and the human voices in our community and our world. As the psalms soak into our bones, they will teach us to listen, not only when we are at prayer, but throughout our whole day, throughout our whole lives. The psalms will teach us to listen with the ear of our hearts—every day.

What else happens to us as we pray the psalms? Demetrius Dumm outlines four characteristics of biblical prayer, especially of the psalms.[13] First of all, the psalms are *incarnational;* they are gutsy. Praying the psalms daily will teach us to be aware of the voice of nature—what is in us and what is around us. The psalms keep before us the very real presence of our own bodies. I complain that my tongue sticks to the roof of my mouth, my throat is dry, my eyes are dim from weeping, I am so wasted that I can count all my bones (see Ps 22:16-18; 31:10; 69:4; 88:10). But our bodies not only complain; they also praise. For example, Psalm 16 says literally, "I bless the Lord who counsels me; even at night my *kidneys* instruct me. . . . So my heart rejoices; my *liver* dances; even my flesh dwells secure" (Ps 16:7, 9).[14] It is impossible to pray the psalms as a disembodied spirit!

The psalms are incarnational in another way: they sound the voices of all creation. We call the trees and rivers to clap their hands, the sea and its creatures to roar, the field and its animals to exult (Ps 96:11-12; 98:7-8). We are in awe of the storm (Ps 29) and the beauty of sun and stars (Ps 8:4; 19:2-7). We ponder God's gift of water: "You make springs gush forth in the valleys; / they flow in between the hills. / They give drink to all the beasts of the field; / the wild asses quench their thirst" (Ps 104:10-11). We are grateful for the gifts of bread and wine to nourish us and warm our hearts (Ps 104:14-15). Every living thing looks to God for food and God provides (Ps 104:27-28). We who pray the psalms become the voice of all creation. Daily we take up our responsibility for the earth.

A second characteristic of the psalms is that they are *historical.* A central belief in the Judeo-Christian tradition is that God works within history—within all the mess of human history. Scripture certainly bears witness to that belief. But the psalms teach us that we not only *tell* our history but also *pray* our history. We pray our history in order to remember, to make present, to bring God's saving deeds of the past into the present so that we might have a future. We pray our past, but this is the *living* word of God, so we also pray ourselves into the future. We will consider this idea in more detail in chapter 2.

A third characteristic of the psalms is that they are *communal*. It is impossible to pray the Psalms alone. You can go in your room and close the door, but by the end of whatever Psalm you pray, we will all be in there with you. If I begin to pray Psalm 130—"Out of the depths I cry to you, O LORD"—I may feel very much alone. But even as I cry out, I find myself speaking not only to God but also to the community: "let Israel hope for the LORD" (Ps 130:1, 7). Another example is Psalm 131, which describes a very intimate moment with God. I rest in God "as a weaned child on its mother." But in the very next verse I find myself saying again, "O Israel, wait for the Lord" (Ps 131:2-3). (In Hebrew the first lines of Pss 130:7 and 131:3 are identical.) In the psalms we go to God together. If I have learned nothing else in my years of studying, teaching, translating, interpreting, and praying, I have learned this: The Bible—and thus the Psalter—is a community book. It is the community who prayed these prayers, kept them, fought over them, translated them, set them to music, and illuminated them. The Psalms are a communal prayer!

Finally, the psalms are *eschatological*; they are open to the future. And yet, they are not eschatological in the sense of a belief in life after death. They are too early for that. The concept of resurrection began to emerge only in the mid-second century BCE. But the psalms do have a strong belief in life. There is a constant prayer to be saved from death and a firm faith that God can and will do this for us. There is a strong conviction that God will eventually make things right—punishing the wicked and blessing the righteous. There is an undying trust that God will take care of each of us: "I believe

I shall see the LORD's goodness / in the land of the living," that is, now in this present life (Ps 27:13). The psalms are open to the future, and we who pray them daily will be open to the future too.

In his 1979 commentary on the psalms, *Runways to God*, Paschal Botz states this as his purpose: "to assist men and women of faith and prayer to become 'psalm happy.' "[15] If we would be happy, this is the *torah* we should ponder night and day. The promise of this *torah* is life. We will be like a tree, planted by a flowing stream, whose leaves do not fade (Ps 1:3). Our liturgical prayer bathes us in the psalms daily. They intersect with every experience of our lives. As John Cassian says, "Thus we shall penetrate its meaning not through the written text but with experience leading the way."[16] The psalms soak into our bones and nourish our roots. We murmur them in hopes that we will be happy. We pray them in hopes that gradually, imperceptibly, like the tree planted by a flowing stream, the same thing will happen to us that Donald Senior said of Carroll Stuhlmueller at his funeral: "This is a person of whom it can truly be said, 'The Word of God became flesh in him.'" This Word of God become flesh in us is the whole rhythm, the ultimate goal of our lives. Then, not only will we be able to sing the first word of the Psalter, "happy"; then we will truly sing the last word of the Psalter: "Let everything that breathes praise the LORD. Alleluia!" (Ps 150:6).

Consider: What do the psalms mean to you? How have they soaked into your bones?

Prayer: Loving God, you who created us with care and breathed into us that we might live, fill us with your Spirit that we may rejoice in your love. This we ask in the name of Jesus, who came that we might have life and have it to the fullest. Amen.

Telling Our Story

I f we pray the psalms, we will become people who understand the essential rhythms of human life. What are those rhythms? I learned a simple way to outline them from Michael Downey, who said that what retreat centers have to offer people is threefold: a place to tell their stories, to cry out their pain, and to sing praise to God.[1] I realized that this rhythm is not only what people find in a retreat; it is the everyday rhythm of the psalms. This chapter and those following expand on that basic rhythm: telling our story, crying out our pain, giving thanks, learning to trust, and singing praise.

We begin by telling our stories. In her book *Diving Deep and Surfacing*, Carol Christ says that telling our stories is essential for our spiritual lives. If we do not tell our stories, we have no tools to help us make significant life decisions. Telling our stories teaches us how to appreciate our whole life's experience, both our struggles and our strengths. The act of telling our stories leads us to understand who we are; "The expression of [our] spiritual quest is integrally related to the telling of [our] stories. If [our] stories are not told, the depth of [our] souls will not be known. Stories give shape to lives."[2]

The psalms help us to tell stories. Despite the fact that the historical psalms (Pss 78, 105, 106, 135, 136) are long and are thus rarely our favorites, an important theological point is being made by those psalms. We learn from the psalms not only to tell our story but also to pray our story. Along the way, we learn that in reality our story is a story about God. In his *Theology of the Old Testament*, Walter Brueggemann says this is what theology is: speech about God—and not just speech but testimony, like the testimony of a witness in court. With Israel, we bear witness to what God has done. To further the courtroom analogy, if the court acts on what a witness says, the witness, in effect, creates reality![3] Reality is dependent on speech. So, by telling the story of God's wonderful works in these Psalms, we are mysteriously speaking them into reality. Do we dare to believe it? Brueggemann says, "the beginning point for articulating an Old Testament theology is in the liturgical, public acknowledgment of a new reality wrought by Yahweh in the life of the speaker and in the community of the speaker."[4] In the testimony we give through the Psalms, we actually describe God, not in statements about "God's character, nature, being, or attributes," but by describing "the concrete, specific actions of God," one at a time.[5]

So what is *our* testimony, the testimony that describes God by God's actions, this testimony that creates reality? We proclaim every time we pray that we do not believe in a god who is static, who lives off on some pink cloud and has nothing to do with the messy, complicated story of our everyday lives. We believe in a God who is in the thick of our story on this very day. We believe in a God who is revealed to us within history:

a God who creates—not outside of time but within it, who actually creates time first, evening and morning, and who sets aside a special time, a day to rest, the seventh day

a God who travels with the ancestors, who has time to be concerned about births and deaths, marriages and barrenness a God who can turn the evil of selling your brother into slavery into the good of redeeming a whole people from starvation

a God who can pay attention to your diet in the desert and the direction of your journey, even if it takes forty years

a God who chooses and unchooses leaders, who chooses the most unlikely, the younger brother, the cheat, the poor speaker, the kid out with the sheep

a God who can begin the journey of providing an anointed messiah for the people even in the midst of the ugly story of adultery, rape, and murder

This is what we bear witness to as we pray the psalms. We do not believe in a god who keeps the divine hands clean and the divine mind uncluttered. We believe in a God who, as Brueggemann says, is passionately concerned with us, who takes sides for us against our enemies, who fights for us and with us, always inexorably leading us toward life. We believe in a God who acts within history, within each of our stories.[6]

This God we believe in is so passionately concerned for our story that finally a divine decision is made to come and join it. The folly of God is certainly greater than human wisdom (1 Cor 1:25)! The Wisdom of God, the Word of God, became flesh and pitched his tent among us (see John 1) and human history will never again be the same. We believe in a God who cares about our history.

God's care for us weaves through all of human history, but we, as individuals, live in such a short piece of it. We weren't there at creation or when God spoke with Abraham. We weren't there to walk through the divided sea or to walk with Jesus. How can we begin to take in all that this wonderful God of history has in mind for us? We tell the story. We remember.

Memory is a very important biblical concept. To remember is to make present; to forget is to cause something or someone to cease to exist. This understanding of memory is not simply about remembering your phone number or the multiplication tables. This is the active taking hold of an event or person and, by the power of your memory, bringing that event or person into the present. We have some experience with that power, I think. When a loved one dies, we tell stories about the person, which is a way of bringing the person back into the present. We also tell stories of the major events in our lives. The telling brings the event back, sometimes quite vividly. Our liturgical worship is based on this power of memory. Liturgists use the Greek term for this power: *anamnesis*. When we do liturgy we gather to tell the story and do the actions in order to remember. Our remembering together brings God's saving actions into our present moment. In the memorial acclamation at Eucharist we proclaim that we remember Christ's death and Christ's resurrection. We also remember his coming in glory. The power of our communal memory brings into one moment God's saving action, not only in the past, but also of the future.

The historical psalms have the same purpose. God's saving acts during the exodus or in the desert were not solely for the generation that happened to be alive at the time. They took place for all of us, for all time. In one version of the Haggadah (the ritual for Passover), our Jewish brothers and sisters begin the Passover celebration by saying:

> With the household of Israel, our elders and young ones, *linking and bonding the past with the future,* we heed once again the divine call to service. *Living our story that is told for all peoples, whose shining conclusion is yet to unfold,* we gather to observe the Passover.[7]

In the *Exsultet* on Holy Saturday night, Christians join the same liturgical public telling of the story of what God did for us, bringing it into the present:

> These, then, are the feasts of *Passover*,
> in which is slain the Lamb, the one true Lamb,
> whose Blood anoints the doorposts of believers.

This is the night,
when once you led our forebears, Israel's children,
from slavery in Egypt
and made them pass dry-shod through the Red Sea.

This is the night,
that with a pillar of fire
banished the darkness of sin.

This is the night
that even now, throughout the world,
sets Christian believers apart from worldly vices
and from the gloom of sin,
leading them to grace
and joining them to his holy ones.[8]

This is the night! No wonder we have to stay up all night at the Easter Vigil! It's a long story, and it's all happening right now!

Psalm 105 teaches us what a gift it is when we do remember. According to this psalm, remembering is high praise. We remember the concrete, specific actions of God, one at a time, and give public, liturgical testimony to the new reality created by God in our lives and in the life of our community. In Psalm 78 we look at the danger of forgetting. This psalm is a whole recital of the people's history, describing what happens if our memories fade. We are warned to tell the wonderful works of God to our children, "that they should set their hope in God, / and never forget God's deeds" (Ps 78:7). Otherwise they will become like our ancestors, "a defiant and rebellious generation" (Ps 78:8). But it seems each generation forgets and God resorts to punishment. Even when we remember that God is our rock (Ps 78:35), we cannot hang on to this security for more than a verse (see Ps 78:36-37, 42). We cannot even remember the wonderful works by which God saved our very lives (Ps 78:42). Forgetting is, according to Psalm 78, the root cause of sin. It is fatal to forget.

We can be grateful that God's memory is better than ours. Even when we forget, God remembers that we are only flesh, a puff of air that is gone in an instant (Ps 78:39). Because God remembers, God is compassionate over and over (Ps 78:38). God's remembering keeps us alive. So we pray in Psalm 25: "Remember your compassion, O LORD, and your faithful love, for they endure forever. Do not remember the sins and rebellions of my youth. Please remember me according to the measure of your faithful love and your goodness, O LORD" (Ps 25:6-7; my translation).

In this psalm, we call on God's remembering in three ways. In the middle, we ask God not to remember the sins of our youth. What God remembers, exists; what God forgets, ceases to be. If God forgets my sins, they no longer exist. Can we learn to believe that? What gives us the courage to make this daring request? We surround this plea with two other appeals to God's memory: "Remember your compassion and love"; "Remember *me* through the lens of your love and goodness." The word for God's compassion (Hebrew, *rahamim*) is based on the Hebrew word for "womb." This is the fierce love of a mother for her child. The word for God's love (Hebrew, *hesed*) means love so deep it has sunk even into one's bones. This is love found in every molecule of one's being. Brueggemann calls *hesed* "tenacious fidelity in a relationship."[9] Finally, we also call on God's goodness. We want God to remember all of those qualities—compassion, love, and goodness—but most of all we want God to remember us! If God calls up the power of divine compassion, love, and goodness while remembering me, I can't lose! All of this divine loving mercy will fill my life.

This mutual remembering connects us to God, the source of our life. Remembering even our troubles somehow redeems the pain by making present God's love that carried us through. Remembering is why and how we do liturgy. We tell God's mighty deeds to make them present in our own lives, to make possible our future. We have to tell the story!

This is what the historical psalms are about, this remembering, this *anamnesis*. But the psalms are not supposed to be the end of the story. Surely they are supposed to encourage us to continue the story. We bear witness: This is what God did at the beginning of time; this is what God did in the thirteenth century BCE; this is what God did after the Babylonian exile. But we Christians do not stop there. As we celebrate Eucharist we remember what God did in Christ at the turn of the era. Even that is not enough. The story has not ended. What is God doing now? How is God creating and redeeming us now? How is the word of God becoming flesh in my life here and now? What is our testimony today?

We pray the historical psalms and then we pray our own story, which is both individual and communal. We are each unique, but none of us goes to God alone. Each of us needs to tell our own story; we also need to tell the story of God's action in our family, our parish, our community, our country, and our world. The storytellers in our midst should be among the most respected persons in the community, even if they repeat the same story over and over. They keep us in touch with God's life in our present time. They midwife the Word becoming flesh in our history today.

We who pray the psalms will be people who know how to tell our story, to bear public liturgical witness. Then, because we are people who listen, we will be able to give others a place and opportunity to tell their stories also, remembering throughout the whole story and always that God's love endures forever.

Consider: What are significant happenings in your own life? How was God present and active at those moments?

Exercise: Praying our Story:

This exercise is designed to help you pray your own story. It can be used individually or in a group.

1. Find Psalm 136 in your Bible or Psalm book.

2. Make a list of several important occurrences in your life—both happy and sad:

   - If you are alone, list happenings in your own life.
   - If you are praying as a family or any group with a shared history, list happenings that apply to the whole group.
   - If you are praying with people who do not have a shared history, ask each person to list 3–5 happenings in his or her own life.

3. Pray verses 1-9 of Psalm 136, answering each invocation with the refrain about God's everlasting love. (In a group, ask one person to be the leader and proclaim the first half of each verse.)

4. After verse 9, insert your own history.

   - If you are alone, continue responding to each event with the refrain.
   - If you are in a group with a shared history, the leader (or someone else) may indicate each event one at a time and the whole group respond with the refrain.
   - If you are in a group without a shared history, divide the assembly into groups of three people each. In each group one person will list the 3–5 significant events and everyone will respond to each with the refrain. Then the second and third persons will do the same. The group responds with the refrain to each event after it is mentioned. All the groups are doing this activity simultaneously.

5. When the recital of events is finished, continue with verses 23-26 of Psalm 136 and respond to each invocation with the refrain.

I have used this exercise many times and the participants are always moved by the experience of praying their own history.

Prayer: God, you who are our past and our future, Alpha and Omega, remember us in your love and keep us always in your present. This we ask in the name of Jesus your son, whose memory is our life. Amen.

Crying Out Our Pain

A significant gift of the psalms is that they teach us how to lament. If we tell our story honestly, we will be led to cry out our pain. If you followed the advice of the previous chapter and took five or ten or fifty events in your life and prayed Psalm 136 with them, you already know that. In our culture we are not good at grieving. We do everything we can to cover up our pain, our weakness, our frailty. Watch the commercials—how many of them have to do with either removing pain or covering up what we consider imperfections? Women have been trained to hide pain. It's not nice to be angry, not polite to complain that we hurt, not holy to long for vengeance against our enemies. But men too have been trained not to cry, not to admit to being wounded, never to acknowledge weakness. We have all been trained not to complain to God; it is unthinkable to shout at God in anger. This is where the laments come in. They give us the words we would never dare say ourselves. (Remember, the psalms are first of all the Word of God!) It's only through genuine lament that we will come to that third step in the rhythm: genuine praise.

The Psalter contains more laments than any other genre. Is this because we pray more when we're in trouble? Or because our sufferings are each unique? Or perhaps just because life is hard? In any case, the structure of the laments teaches us how to deal with difficulty: take it straight to God. There is no skulking in corners in the lament. We cry out clearly and powerfully about whatever is troubling us: sorrow, pain, enemies, and even death. Nothing is too raw to be brought to God in prayer!

Laments are *addressed* directly to God. We take our complaint straight to the top! "My God, my God, why have you forsaken me?" (Ps 22:2). "Hear, O God, the voice of my complaint" (Ps 64:1). "Have mercy on me, O God" (Ps 51:3). "Save me, O God, for the waters / have risen to my neck" (Ps 69:2). "I called, the God of justice gave me answer; / from anguish you released me, have mercy and hear me!" (Ps 4:2).

After our cry to God, our lament may go in several directions. Like our lives when we are lamenting, the elements are often all mixed up. Lamenting is not neat! Some of the themes or movements we find in laments are a complaint, a description of suffering, a prayer for help, a motivation for God, a promise, or a vow.

In case we do not have our own list of *complaints* (or do not know how to express them), the laments express every possible distress we can imagine. We are sick: our bones are disjointed and our tongue sticks to the roof of our mouths (Ps 22:15-16). Even our friends have turned against us (Ps 41:10; 55:14-15). Enemies lay snares for us and pierce us with bitter words (Ps 64:4-6). We know our guilt (Ps 51:5) and we know God sees it (Ps 90:8). We are in the pits (Ps 130:1). We say over and over to God, "How long?" Whatever your complaint, there's a lament for you!

In our *prayer for help* we tell God what we want—and often how we want God to do it. We ask God to rescue us, to come quickly to help us, to heal us, to grant us justice (Ps 6:3-5;

40:14; 43:1). Over and over we ask God to hear us (e.g., Ps 4:2; 17:1; 28:2; 30:11). We want God to rain burning coals on our enemies, to let them fall into the traps they have set for us, to make them dissolve like a slug in the sun, and to let death surprise them (Ps 140:11; 57:7; 58:9; 55:16). For ourselves, we want God to answer us and give light to our eyes (Ps 13:4). Are you shocked? Remember that these psalms are, first of all, God's word to us!

Some of these prayers may resonate with our own experience. When I was a child, I used to be rewarded for picking the slugs off of the growing tomato plants in the garden. Somewhere I learned that if salt is poured on a slug, it will disappear. Actually, the poor slug virtually evaporates! I don't know how many slugs I put to a painful death. At that point in my life I did not have much awareness of our common unity as creatures of God. But I do know what it means to dissolve like a slug in the sun!

We *motivate* God to help us by pointing out that God has covenant obligations to us (never mind that we may have forgotten ours). We remind God of what God did in the past:

> We heard with our own ears, O God;
> our forebears have declared to us
> the things you did in their days,
> you yourself, in days long ago. . . .
> Yet now you have rejected us, disgraced us;
> you no longer go forth with our armies. (Ps 44:2, 10)

Paradoxically we say either, "I'm guilty, so have mercy on me" (see Ps 51) or, "I'm innocent, so vindicate me" (see Ps 17). We cannot lose! We suggest to God that letting us suffer will ruin God's reputation (see Ps 42–43). Interestingly, we learned this from Moses. In the golden calf incident, when God threatens to destroy Israel, Moses challenges God: "What will the Egyptians say?" We remind God that we are the ones who give praise. We say, "You will miss me if I die!" (see Pss 6 and 88). We make promises or vows to God: "If you get me out of this, I'll offer you a nice fat sheep." The modern equivalent may be, "I'll say the rosary every day!" or, "I'll fast three times a week!"

All of that expression of distress is going on—somewhat jumbled up—in the middle section of a lament after we have cried out to God. But the *final section* of the lament is usually a turn to hope. Laments almost always *end* in confidence and thanksgiving. Perhaps this assurance results from God's answer to the sufferer expressed in the words of a priest or prophet. Some psalms contain such an oracle:

> I will hear what the LORD God speaks;
> he speaks of peace for his people and his faithful,
> and those who turn their hearts to him. (Ps 85:9)

> A voice I did not know said to me:
> "I freed your shoulder from the burden;
> your hands were freed from the builder's basket."
> (Ps 81:6-7)

Or perhaps, as Demetrius Dumm suggests, the assurance is simply in the spirit of David, the cry of an unquenchable faith.[1] Dumm also says that "we do not bother to complain to someone who does not love us!"[2]

A simple way to look at the lament psalms is to consider our three basic relationships: ourselves, others, and God. At some point each of these relationships confronts us with *the enemy. God* is the enemy in Psalm 88:

> You have laid me in the depths of the pit,
> in regions that are dark and deep.
> Your anger weighs down upon me;
> I am drowned beneath your waves.
> You have taken away my friends;
> to them you have made me hateful. (Ps 88:7-9)

Our own sin is the enemy in Psalm 51: "My transgressions, truly I know them; / my sin is always before me" (Ps 51:5). Or as another translation puts it: "I know my evil well, / it stares me in the face."[3] We all remember the psalms where *other people* are the enemy: scandalous liars, the arrogant, those who wait in ambush to attack us: "For dogs have surrounded me; / a band of the wicked besets me" (Ps 22:17).

Let us look first at Psalm 51, which is everyone's favorite penitential psalm. It is the clearest example of a psalm in which, as Pogo used to say, "we have met the enemy and it is us." Perhaps best of all the psalms, Psalm 51 captures our pleading for forgiveness and our hope for a new beginning. It really is one of the most hopeful prayers in the psalter.

Psalm 51 begins with a title, a little meditation added by an ancient editor to help us get into the spirit of the psalm. Like many of the other psalm titles, this one too is about David, "when the prophet Nathan came to him after he had gone to Bathsheba." Now we probably are not often in David's situation, guilty of adultery and murder, but there is still wisdom to be gleaned from this title.

First of all, the seriousness of David's crimes and the hopefulness of the psalm tell us that there is nothing too horrible for God to forgive. Nothing. We are often more stingy with forgiveness than God is, so we assume that God will be slow to forgive too. The psalm teaches us that this is not true. Second, our ancient editor places this psalm *after* Nathan the prophet speaks to David. Nathan has told David a parable, a story of a little loved ewe lamb taken from its owner by a selfish neighbor to feed a guest. With the parable Nathan draws David into pronouncing judgment against himself: "The man who has done this deserves to die." Nathan replies, "You are the man!" (see 2 Sam 12:5–7). It takes Nathan's story to make David aware of his guilt. Blindness to guilt is also true of us more often than we like to admit. We can get very good at hiding our sinfulness from ourselves. Only when someone else calls us on it does our transgression "stare us in the face" (Ps 51:5). The confrontation between David and Nathan is a model for us: Nathan is wonderfully gentle. He only tells a story. David is wonderfully humble. He does not make excuses. He says simply, "I have sinned against the Lord" (2 Sam 12:13). Nathan replies with equal simplicity, "The Lord has put away your sin." But sin, even after it is acknowledged and forgiven, still has consequences. The child will die. David's example of rape and murder will be followed by his children. His son Amnon rapes his half-sister (David's daughter) Tamar. Tamar's full brother Absalom murders Amnon (2 Sam 13). We hear of David as a model of repentance, fasting, and weeping, but sometimes we forget that he was not fasting and weeping for himself but for his children who suffer because of his sin.

Psalm 51 begins, like most laments, with a cry directly to God. We call out with four imperatives: have mercy, blot out, wash, cleanse. Actually, the third imperative is, literally, "make a lot of washings." We might translate it as "scrub." Most translators prefer a gentler verb, perhaps a maternal image. But who scrubbed you? Wasn't it your mother? The cry also has a wonderful balance. There are three Hebrew words for sin: *pesha'* (rebellion), *'awon* (guilt), *hatta'* (sin). And there are three words for God's mercy: *hanan* (mercy, favor), *hesed* (faithful covenant love, love in the bones), and *rahamim* (womb love—this really is God our mother). We use the whole vocabulary for sin to say, "You name it God! I've done it!" But the powerful words for mercy convince us that God can and will make us whole again. Psalm 51 adds together our sinfulness and God's mercy and comes out with the answer: God scrubs us clean.

The middle section of the psalm consists of a description of our distress and a petition. It is here that we admit we are our own worst enemy by saying, "I know my evil well; it stares me in the face." We acknowledge that if God condemns us, God would be in the right! We say this in truth, knowing that God does not owe us mercy; rather, it is always a gift. We also say this in absolute freedom, confident of God's constant inclination to forgive.

After this admission, we begin our petition: teach me, cleanse me (literally, "un-sin me"), wash me. Turn away your face from the sin that stares me in the face. Take away the sin that destroys my body, crushes my bones. Let my bruised bones dance. Let me rejoice again (see Ps 51:9-11). But this petition is only the introduction to the boldest request of all. Right at the center of the psalm we take our courage in hand and beg of God: "Create a pure heart for me, O God; / renew a steadfast spirit within me" (Ps 51:12). We are not asking God to just forgive and forget. We ask, "Make me new and start from the very center of my being." This is total surrender to God. This is our way of dealing with the enemy that is ourselves. We beg, "Make me new!"

Are we really willing to be created anew? Is that why we ask again for a willing spirit? Is that why our sacrifice is a broken spirit, a broken, humbled heart (Ps 51:19)? It is not easy to trust God this much. It is not easy to let the potter start over with the clay. Looking ahead, this is why I think the resurrection is Jesus' greatest act of obedience—and ours too! It is total surrender to God's gift of life, to God's creating hand.

The psalm draws to a conclusion after we have surrendered to God's creative hand. Now we are driven back to the community. When we make our vow of praise, we know that we cannot fulfill it alone. Jesus is again our model. As soon as God raises him from the dead, he is back in the midst of the disciples, teaching them, eating with them, calling them to forgive one another, sending them out, and promising to be with them always. Being created new doesn't mean we get to sit down and enjoy it! Immediately in Psalm 51 we are promising to teach the wicked, to bring sinners back to God, to sing unending praise to our loving God. This absolute openness of our hearts to God is the true meaning of sacrifice. All sacrifice has as its purpose union with God, whether sharing life with God by eating with God (the idea behind most of Israel's sacrifice and our own Eucharist) or the total surrender of life to God in trust (the whole burnt offering, the martyrs, the cross, and monastic profession). Our sacrifice is a heart broken open, totally cleansed, totally given.

Someone (probably a liturgist!) got hold of Psalm 51 and was afraid that prayer would become so spiritualized that we would stop gathering to do it, that we would stop bringing our best to share with God, and that we would forget prayer has something to do with bodies and with the rest of our material world. So this liturgist added two verses (20-21) about genuine liturgical worship, when our hearts and bodies are one and we sanctify the good gifts of the world around us by using them to help us worship God. Then God will be pleased with our sacrifice.

There are four things to remember from Psalm 51, our acknowledgment that we are our own worst enemies:

- First, we should place absolute trust in God's merciful love. Nothing, absolutely nothing, can separate us from the love of God. That is what Jesus came to show us and David already knew.

- Second, this psalm gives us the courage to be honest— simply, humbly honest. I know my evil well, but I also know that I can teach others and bring them back to God. I know that my heart, broken open, is a delight to God.

- Third, Psalm 51 calls us daily to surrender to the creative hand of God—a little practice for resurrection, if you will. This is tough. Surrendering to life in all the ways it shapes us and breaks us open is never easy. It takes a brave person to say to God, "Create in me a clean heart, a new spirit."

- Finally, Psalm 51 calls us to give flesh to the good news: to let our bruised bones dance; to teach and sing God's praise with lips, tongue, mouth; and to bring the rest of the created world to offer praise with us, such as flowers, bread, wine, wood, pottery, candles, gold and silver, cloth and glass and paper, reeds and pipes, strings and cymbals. By including all the good gifts that share the planet with us in prayer, we shall offer proper sacrifice to this amazing God who loves us so much that we can hardly imagine it, much less believe it.

Exercise: When the enemy is myself:

1. Consider your own frailty—your faults, your sinfulness, the things you wish you had not done or said. Be honest but gentle with yourself. This is an exercise in hope rather than in blaming.

2. Cry out directly to God: "God, hurry and help me," or "Lord, hear my cry and answer me," or "How long, O Lord!"

3. Tell God your trouble. Don't be shy!
    - Describe your pain.
    - Complain!
    - Give God reasons to help you: God has helped you (or others) in the past; it's in God's nature to help; other people will see and praise God for helping you; no one can help you but God.
    - Make promises; bargain with God!
    - Say whatever is on your mind: God can take it!

4. Turn to hope. Thank God for listening, for helping, for always being present. And don't forget to keep the promises you made!

Prayer: Loving God, you sent your Son to share our pain that we might share your life; hear us now as we tell you our troubles. Heal our hearts and minds and bodies, we beg you. This we ask in the name of Jesus, who is our hope and our joy. Amen.

Dealing with Our Enemies

We are usually most comfortable with recognizing ourselves as the enemy. Indeed, we have learned to acknowledge our own sinfulness, and we know that sometimes we are our own worst enemies. Our other two types of relationships are more difficult. We cringe at the violent *curses* hurled toward human enemies. We are even more uncomfortable flinging accusations in the face of God. But biblical prayer is not nice!

What can the laments possibly teach us about praying, especially in this violent language? Consider the psalms in which we "curse" other people. Notice first that, rather than attacking enemies ourselves, we *leave the exercise of vengeance to God*. Isn't it better to ask God to crush the enemies' teeth in their mouths than to go out and do it ourselves? If we reflect, we already know what God will do! Remember how angry Jonah was when God forgave the hated Ninevites? He explained that he didn't want to leave home in the first place because he "knew that you are a gracious God and merciful, slow to anger and abounding in steadfast love" (see Jonah 4:2). In the end, God will forgive our enemies if we let God take the responsibility. (Maybe that's really why we do not want to pray these psalms! We are afraid God might forgive our awful enemies!)

Second, by outwardly expressing through prayer *the violence that nests in every human heart,* we can rob the violence of its power. When I was a young sister, fresh out of graduate school, I was assigned to teach a course on the Psalter to our older sisters. I know now that the real purpose of the assignment was for the older sisters to teach me what the psalms really meant. But together we went on bravely until we came to the "cursing" psalms. One venerable sister exclaimed, "I can't say those things in church!" Thinking that from years of monastic life she had probably worked the violence out of her heart, I was ready to say, "Oh, Sister, you don't need to say them." But before I could open my mouth, one of her contemporaries blurted out, "I don't know why you can't say them in church. You say them in the hall!" I've never forgotten this lesson: violence sticks in our hearts for a very long time! Through the lament psalms we are enabled to acknowledge, and thus to let go of, our very real anger and hatred.

Another way we can deal with these psalms is to consider *what (or who) my/our enemies are.* Often someone will say to me, "How can you pray those awful baby-bashing psalms?" (Ps 137:9). I learned how to pray Psalm 137 from St. Benedict, who learned it from Origen, a theologian of the third century.[1] Benedict (following Origen) knew that our true enemies are our own sinful thoughts: "As soon as wrongful thoughts come into your heart, dash them against Christ" (*RB* 4.50). He teaches us to resist temptations while they are still babies and bash them against the rock who is Christ (*RB* Prol. 28). This is how to pray Psalm 137!

What about Psalm 109? If you are looking for curses, this is your best list. But who are the enemies I can pray against here? Consider Psalm 109:15: Let "their memory be cut off from the earth." Can I pray that against poverty, homelessness, drug abuse, terrorist bombings? Can I pray against war: "Let the days of [its] life be few . . . in a generation [its] name blotted out" (Ps 109:8, 13)? Or I might pray Psalm 58 against Alzheimer's disease, cancer, AIDS: "Before they put forth thorns, like a bramble / let them be swept away, green wood or dry!" (Ps 58:10). This is not cheating or ignoring the meaning of the psalm! This is how Christians from the beginning have been praying these psalms, just as Benedict learned from his predecessor, Origen.

Another aid to praying these difficult psalms are *psalm collects*, prayers that are sometimes found at the end of each psalm. These collects are very useful for *lectio divina*. John Cassian, a monk who lived in the fifth century, describes the practice of desert monks.[2] One monk would recite a psalm; following this, all would pray in silence. Then one person would "collect" the silent reflection of the community in a prayer. These psalm collects flourished between the fourth and seventh centuries and have been revived in the current Roman Liturgy of the Hours. Their main purpose seems to have been the adaptation of the psalms to Christian truths. For example, let us look at Psalm 109, perhaps the most difficult for any believer. Below are collects for Psalm 109 from three ancient collections: a Roman collection from the fifth to sixth century, a Spanish series from sometime before the eighth century, and an African series from the fifth century. Following these is my own collect.

Roman: "God of singular mercy, you who deigned to bear the curse so that you might root out from us the curse of the law, we beseech you to act toward us mercifully according to your name, deign to free us both from being overtaken by vice and also from the disparagement of evil."[3]

Spanish: "Deal with us mercifully, Lord, according to your name, for what is more sweet, than that through which you free us from death and join us to yourself everlastingly, through which you fill our need and in holy abundance without any lack you allow us to remain there? Grant that it may make us acceptable, you who have reconciled us who were your enemies."[4]

African: "Made heirs of your blessing, Lord, we may not fear the curses of your enemies. Although they have spoken evil against my soul, you, Lord, O Lord, help me according to your great mercy."[5]

Nowell: "God of justice, rescuer of the poor, root out evil from the world, that we, who deserve accusation, may learn to imitate your mercy. This we ask in the name of your Son, who, being innocent, overcame evil with good."

All three collects in the older series use the psalm phrase, "deal with us mercifully," which is one of the few positive notes in the psalm. The three older collects each treat the problem of evil differently. The Roman collect recalls Jesus' identification with evildoers and asks to be freed from being overtaken by evil. The enemy is "the law," as well as our own tendency to sin. We also fear attack. The Spanish collect asks for reconciliation. The enemies are death, our own need, and the recognition that we ourselves have been God's enemies. The African collect is the most literal of the three. We ask to be freed from fear of enemies, but we also consider our enemies to be God's enemies. My collect is an attempt to incorporate the idea of overcoming evil with good. Perhaps you might wish to write your own, in order to find a way to pray this psalm against the enemies outside us.

Yet another way to deal with the laments is to regard the example of our ancestors in the faith and *to relate the laments to other biblical stories*. The titles of the psalms show us how to relate the laments to other stories. Many of the laments are connected through the titles with incidents in the life of David. For example, the superscription to Psalm 3 says, "A Psalm of David, as he is fleeing from his son Absalom." Reading the tragic story of David's relationship with his son in 2 Samuel 15–19 helps to bring the lament to life. We can create our own superscriptions, our own connections between the Psalms and the rest of the biblical story. Beth LaNeel Tanner reads Psalm 109 in the voices of Leah and Rachel when their father Jacob ruins both of their weddings.[6] The use of the laments with the biblical stories in the Roman Lectionary for Eucharist is another example of this method. For example, after we hear Jeremiah's complaint against God on the Twelfth Sunday of Year A, we sing Psalm 69. The refrain is nice: "Lord, in your great love, answer me." But if we look at the whole psalm, we discover that it begins, "Save me, O God, for the waters / have risen to my neck." We recall Jeremiah's suffering in the muddy cistern (Jer 38:4-13) and sing the psalm in his voice.

Finally, we might pray Psalm 109 with the psalm book in one hand and the daily newspaper in the other. We have a responsibility to bring to God the pain and anger of those who suffer along with our own feelings. They are the poor at whose right hand God stands (Ps 109:31). I have done this with groups of students. I frequently take the morning paper (any day will do) and cut the front page into sections. After dividing the students into groups I give each group a front-page story and instruct them to write a lament. They must first decide in whose voice they will pray. Then they construct a lament with an initial cry to God, a middle section, and a turn to hope. The results are inspiring. One group, who had the story of a massacre in Borneo, including a picture of a woman fleeing with a baby in her arms, ended their lament in the tone of Psalm 137: "May someone do to your babies what you are doing to ours." They said, "We hate that psalm! But how else could we cry out in this woman's name?" Another group used the description of the temple destruction in Psalm 74 as a model for their lament over the destruction of the Buddhist statues in Afghanistan. A third group had the story of a mass grave found in Chechnya. Surprisingly, they decided to pray in the voice of the perpetrators, those who had killed the victims. They concluded their lament with this prayer: "Give me what I could not give; O God, have mercy on me." Elizabeth Johnson talks about our need not only to sympathize with the poor and suffering but to cry out in their voice.[7] I am convinced that refusing to pray the psalms of lament is a refusal to pray in the voice of the poor, to give voice to the voiceless sufferers.

The psalms give us words to deal with the enemy outside of us. But what can we do when the enemy is God? We take refuge in the example of Job who complains against God through all his suffering. He says terrible things, and yet he is declared by God to be the only one who speaks rightly (Job 42:8). Why? Because he is the only one who speaks *to* God. Everyone else in the story only talks *about* God. Jeremiah too complains against God and yet remains faithful. Moses also says some pretty brave things to God: "If this is the way you are going to treat me, put me to death at once" (Num 11:15). There are other examples in Scripture of courageous prayer. A good example is Psalm 88.

Psalm 88 begins with a cry to God. In fact, the cry to God is at the beginning (v. 2), in the middle (v. 10), and toward the end (v. 14). All day we cry to God, and we will not let God forget it! The description of distress is simple: I am in deepest distress, close to death, and, God, it's all your fault! You plunged me into the bottom of the pit; your wrath lies heavy upon me; your waves crash over me; you took away my friends.

But the middle section adds a new idea. In a series of questions, the psalmist challenges God: Do you work wonders for the dead? What happens in the grave? If I die, will you be able to do anything about it? The psalmist is sure that the answer is: "No. God is a god of the living. God is not present in the shadowy realm of the dead." The questions are meant as motivation to God: Save me now, while you have the chance! If I die it will be too late! Then who will praise you? Then you'll be sorry!

The last section returns to the complaint: You have done this, God. Why? There is nothing left for me but darkness. This lament, unlike almost all others, ends in darkness. There is no vow of praise, no thanksgiving for help that we know is on the way, no expression of confidence in God. Psalm 88 does not let God off the hook. This psalm is not for the weak! We end this psalm as if to say: Now it's your move, God.

Psalm 88 seems to have no turn to hope, but perhaps the very cry itself is a turn to hope! Bruce Vawter tells a Yiddish story that illustrates that hope:

> On the eve of Yom Kippur, the most solemn and sacred day, an old Jew looked up to heaven and sighed: "Dear God, listen: I, Herschel the tailor, put it to You! The butcher in our village, Shepsel, is a good man, an honorable man, who never cheats anyone and always gives full weight, and never turns away the needy; yet Shepsel himself is so poor that he and his wife sometimes go without meat! . . . Or take Fishel, our shoemaker, a model of piety and kindness—yet his beloved mother is dying in terrible pain. . . . And Reb Label, our *melamed* (teacher), who loves all the lads he teaches and is loved by all who know him—lives hand to mouth, hasn't a decent suit to his name, and just developed an eye disease that may leave him blind! . . . So, on this most holy night, I ask You directly, God: Is this *fair*? I repeat: Is this *fair*? . . . So, tomorrow, O Lord, on our sacred Yom Kippur—if You forgive us, we will forgive You!"[8]

Accusations against God are *an expression of faith*. We challenge God because we believe that God has the power to relieve our distress. Therefore we cry, "Hurry up!" We challenge God because our only hope is to cling to that relationship even when God seems to be absent, and so we cry, "Wake up!" It is a courageous faith, which clings to God through the absurdity of suffering. It is a faith that God cannot resist.

Even though the laments may make us uneasy (or perhaps because they do), the lament is a healthy prayer. It is given to us that we might learn how to live in a world of suffering and injustice, neither being conquered by evil nor abandoning hope in God. The evils that attack our lives are laid clearly before God. Our feelings of helpless bitterness are acknowledged honestly. We acknowledge that only God can conquer evil. We pray every day in the Lord's Prayer: "Deliver us from evil." The laments expand on that central prayer. Our perseverance in lament continues to persuade God to redeem the world.

Consider: What is your lament? What grief, what pain? How do you lament for the sufferings of the world?

Exercise: When the enemy is outside of myself
This exercise is designed to help you deal with the enemies that threaten us.

1. Look at the front page of today's paper and choose a story that tells of a tragedy or danger.

2. There will usually be several voices in the story. Decide in whose voice you will pray; for example, you may choose the victim(s), perpetrator(s), bystanders, or the relatives and friends of any party.

3. Construct your lament:
   - Cry out to God. Use whatever names of God you wish and ask God to hear you.
   - Cry out against the "enemy": Describe the distress of the person(s) in whose voice you are praying. Complain; make promises to God; try to persuade God. Perhaps you may even want to pray for vengeance!
   - Ask God to remedy the situation and heal the sufferers.

4. Turn to hope: Praise and thank God for listening to you and the person in whose voice you pray.

5. If you wish, you may also want to write a psalm collect.

Prayer: Compassionate God, you who love all things you have made, protect us from our enemies and open our hearts to forgive all who have hurt us. Touch us in your love, that we may be strengthened and consoled. This we ask in the name of Jesus, by whose wounds we are healed. Amen.

Giving Thanks

et me stir your memories, or at least your imagination, a little. Think of a time when you were very sick, perhaps in great pain. Do you remember the moment when the pain stopped and you knew you were going to get well? Or think of the moment when your body stiffened at the awareness you were going to have a car accident—and then miraculously the accident didn't happen. How did you feel at that moment? Someone has said, "The moment after pain is the sweetest upon earth." If you capture that emotion you will understand the songs of thanksgiving.

The fragile moment of rescue is the seedbed for the song of thanksgiving. We are afraid to move or even breathe lest the danger or pain return. There is a strong awareness of dependence on God for everything—life, breath, relief from pain, joy. There is a thin-skinned emotion in the songs of thanksgiving. Joy is heightened because of the memory of recent pain; praise is rich because of the knowledge of recent helplessness.

These psalms resemble the final section of many laments. But there is an important difference: in the lament, deliverance is anticipated, whereas in the song of thanksgiving, deliverance has just been experienced.

Because they are so close to the lament, these psalms often describe both the distress and the deliverance. God not only answers our cry for help but answers on the very day we call and silences the anger of our enemies (Ps 138:3, 7; 120:1). Even though they pressed us hard from our youth, they could never overcome us (Ps 129:2). We bless God, "who did not give us / a prey to their teeth!" (Ps 124:6). God not only does away with our enemies but also makes our land fruitful and our harvests abundant (Ps 65:10-15). Most important of all, God forgives our sin (Ps 32:1-2). "At night come tears, but dawn brings joy" (Ps 30:6). We walk with the Lord in this land of the living (Ps 116:9).

How do these psalms teach us to give thanks? First, in order to show how great is God's rescue, we have to tell how great was our distress. Psalm 18 is a good example of this immediacy, of the nearness of pain. It begins with bold thanksgiving:

> I love you, Lord, my strength;
> O Lord, my rock, my fortress, my savior;
> my God, my rock where I take refuge;
> my shield, my saving strength, my stronghold.
> I cry out, "Praised be the Lord!"
> and see, I am saved from my foes. (Ps 18:2-4)

See how secure we are? But we haven't forgotten the pain:

> The waves of death rose about me;
> the torrents of destruction assailed me;
> the snares of the grave surrounded me;
> the traps of death confronted me. (Ps 18:5-6)

We remember the lament as well as its consequences:

> In my anguish I called to the Lord;
> I cried to my God for help.

From his temple he heard my voice;
my cry to him reached his ears. (Ps 18:7)

Our feelings are very close to the surface and often alternate between fear and delight. We were helpless. We knew it. Only God could rescue us and—how can we believe it!—God did!

A few stories will illustrate this emotional seesaw. Beryl Schewe, one of my students, wrote a thanksgiving psalm about the birth of her daughter Sarah. She chose Psalm 116 as her model. The beginning of her psalm is clearly a lament as she cries out in anguish and anger. Her final shout, as her husband encourages her to "push," is: "More? You want more?" Then, as the child is born, the psalm turns immediately to thanksgiving as she exclaims, "Oh, beautiful, bloody child!"[1] The thanksgiving overwhelms the agony. As Jesus remarks, "she no longer remembers the anguish because of the joy of having brought a human being into the world" (John 16:21). Another student also used Psalm 116 as the pattern for a young refugee's thanksgiving. This young woman had been captured and tortured in her native country, and forced to fight for a cause she did not believe in. Eventually she was freed and brought to the United States. Her thanksgiving tells the story of her torture clearly, but there is no bitterness in it. She too turns in thanksgiving to God for her rescue and all the blessings that came with it.

This third story was told to me by a friend. He was living in a small Kansas town and had driven into Kansas City to go to the symphony with a friend. As he started home after the concert it began to rain and Interstate 70 became slick. Then it happened: he slid off the road into the ditch. He had already begun thanking God that he wasn't hurt and hadn't hit anyone when a trucker stopped to help. The trucker surveyed the situation, offered to call the highway patrol, and left. When the patrol officer arrived, he too checked the situation, called a tow truck, and left. My friend had now added to his thanksgiving a prayer for all those who came to his assistance. The tow truck came and pulled him out of the ditch. Then he also prepared to leave. My friend said, "You're not going to leave me too, are you?" The driver answered, "You're OK. The car is out of the ditch, and your insurance covers the tow. You can now drive home! Yes, I'm going to leave." All the way home my friend kept praying, "O God, don't let me slide into the ditch again!" (Note: he's back to lament!) In the morning he went out to look at his car and saw only one small scratch. Then his thanksgiving returned with energy! He could have prayed Psalm 40, where the pain is so close that the song of thanksgiving turns into a lament by verse 13: "For I am beset with evils / too many to be counted." But by the last verse the thanksgiving is back: "Wretched and poor though I am, / the Lord is mindful of me" (Ps 40:18). The moment of thanksgiving is very fragile and the lament is not forgotten.

The bottom line is always that we are threatened with death and God saves us. Psalm 116 begins with a strong declaration of love.

> I love the Lord, for he has heard
> my voice, my appeal;
> for he has turned his ear to me
> whenever I call. (Ps 116:1-2)

The Hebrew line actually says simply, "I love, because the Lord has heard me!" Haven't you had that experience? God rescues you from some disaster or danger and your heart overflows with love for everyone and everything? Robert Davidson sees this rush of love as God's gift: "We love because he first loved us" (1 John 4:19).[2] But even in that moment of grateful love, we cannot forget the terror. We quote the lament and then describe God's wonderful goodness.

> They surrounded me, the snares of death;
> the anguish of the grave has found me;

> anguish and sorrow I found.
> I called on the name of the LORD:
> "Deliver my soul, O LORD!"
>
> How gracious is the LORD, and just;
> our God has compassion.
> The LORD protects the simple;
> I was brought low, and he saved me.
>
> Turn back, my soul, to your rest,
> for the LORD has been good to you;
> he has kept my soul from death,
> my eyes from tears, and my feet from stumbling.
> I will walk in the presence of the LORD
> in the land of the living. (Ps 116:3-9)

We remember that we never gave up hope in God. We were desperate but we couldn't let go of God. Now, in our joy at being rescued, we want to express our thanks in a tangible way.

> I trusted, even when I said,
> "I am sorely afflicted,"
> and when I said in my alarm,
> "These people are all liars."
>
> How can I repay the LORD
> for all his goodness to me?
> The cup of salvation I will raise;
> I will call on the name of the LORD.
>
> My vows to the LORD I will fulfill
> before all his people. (Ps 116:10-14)

Immediately following this assertion of confidence and desire to repay God, we pray a verse that seems confusing: "How precious in the eyes of the LORD / is the death of his faithful" (Ps 116:15). Does this imply that God enjoys our death? No! It is just the opposite! We have already declared "the Lord has been good . . . has kept my soul from death" (Ps 116:7b-8a). God hasn't suddenly changed the divine mind and decided to do away with us! This cannot be true!

Why, then, do we pray verse 15 for the feasts of martyrs and at funerals? Certainly not because we think the death of these people is good. Rather, we have faith that they still live! We believe in the resurrection. But the psalmist didn't have a glimmer of insight that there was any life after our time on earth. So what does this verse mean? What would it have meant to the psalmist? How could our death be "precious" to God? We have to probe deeper. The verse is saying that our death is too "pricey" for God. It is "precious" in the sense that it costs too much. We used to use the word "dear" in that way, like the German word *teuer*.

A story of one of our German-born sisters in charge of the kitchen illustrates this meaning of *teuer*. She was outraged that the butcher had raised the price of meat so she declared to him: "You are dearer to me now than when first we met!" Sadly, no one remembers the response of the butcher! I hope someone explained to him that "dear" could also mean "expensive"!

We proclaim Psalm 116:15 because our faith tells us it is too costly for God to let us die. It is so costly that God came to share in our suffering and death in order to defeat death once and for all. We have been "bought with a price" (1 Cor 6:20). "Where, O death, is your victory? Where, O death, is your sting?" (1 Cor 15:55). More than the psalmist ever knew, God saves us from death. We pray the psalms of thanksgiving with added intensity because of our Christian faith!

Another element in our thanksgiving is storytelling. In order to give thanks, we must tell the story of our experience, of our danger. There must be stories. Don't you experience this? A friend or relative hits a deer. Then the breathtaking story of the crash must be told over and over—on the phone, at a meal, on the road—until you can recite it yourself. The repetition of the story may be annoying, but our moments of deliverance must be told. Usually we can hardly wait to tell them! It's instinctive.

We tell the story to give thanks to God. In Psalm 40 we declare:

> Your justice I have proclaimed
> in the great assembly.
> My lips I have not sealed;
> you know it, O LORD.
>
> Your saving help I have not hidden in my heart;
> of your faithfulness and salvation I have spoken.
> I made no secret of your merciful love
> and your faithfulness to the great assembly. (Ps 40:10-11)

In Psalm 66 we call out to all believers: "Come and hear, all who fear God; / I will tell what he did for my soul" (Ps 66:16). In Psalm 107 we give the assembly a verse to sing with us:

> "O give thanks to the LORD for he is good;
> for his mercy endures forever."
> Let the redeemed of the LORD say this,
> those he redeemed from the hand of the foe,
> and gathered from far-off lands,
> from east and west, north and south. (Ps 107:1-3)

Psalm 107 is a wonderful example of a thanksgiving liturgy. This is my vision of the action that accompanies the psalm. Many people want to give thanks for the way God has rescued them from danger during the past year. So a thanksgiving liturgy is planned. The congregation is gathered and the liturgist has organized the grateful people into five groups: those who wandered in the desert, those who were imprisoned, those who were sick, those who were in peril on the sea, and those whose crops failed. After every group tells its story the assembly sings a refrain: "Let them thank the

Lord for his mercy" (Ps 107:8, 15, 21, 31). The celebration ends with a meditation on the wisdom of giving thanks:

> The upright see it and rejoice,
> while all the wicked close their mouths.
> Should not one who is wise recall these things,
> and understand the merciful deeds of the Lord?
>
> (Ps 107:42-43)

Thus our telling of the story encourages others. It's part of our testimony to God's goodness:

> He put a new song into my mouth,
> praise of our God.
> Many shall see and fear
> and shall trust in the Lord. (Ps 40:4)

> You have changed my mourning into dancing,
> removed my sackcloth and girded me with joy.
> So my soul sings psalms to you, and will not be silent.
> O Lord my God, I will thank you forever. (Ps 30:12-13)

Because the thanksgiving is on the way from lament to praise, we are a little confused about the receiver of our words. Like the lament, most songs of thanksgiving are addressed to God: "I will praise you, Lord, with all my heart" (9:2). "I love you, Lord, my strength" (18:2). "I will extol you, Lord, for you have raised me up" (30:2). "Praise is due to you / in Sion, O God" (65:2). But then we get started with the story and we need an audience, more people to help us give thanks. It happens again and again. You can almost see the turn. In Psalm 30 we are speaking to God in verse 4 and to the congregation in verse 5:

> O Lord, you have lifted up my soul from the grave,
> restored me to life from those who sink into the pit.
> Sing psalms to the Lord, you faithful ones;
> give thanks to his holy name. (Ps 30:4-5)

Even the vocabulary teaches us that thanksgiving requires the gathering of an audience. The Hebrew word for "thanks" (*ydh*, noun *todah*) also means "praise." It makes an interesting contrast to the lament: We go straight to God to complain, but in order to give thanks we have to round up someone else so we can tell how wonderful God is! If only we did that with each other! Too often we round up others only to talk about how terrible someone is, or we drag the generous person off into a corner to whisper, "Thanks."

Not only do we gather a crowd; we have a party! We bring all these folks to the sanctuary for a celebration. A good example of this is Psalm 118, our great Easter Psalm, which gives us the popular verse, "This is the day the Lord has made," for the great alleluia at the Easter Vigil and the response for both Easter Sunday and the Second Sunday of Easter ABC. Obviously what we are doing during the Easter season is giving thanks! In Psalm 118 we first call people with a little litany:

> Give praise to the LORD, for he is good;
> his mercy endures forever.
>
> Let the house of Israel say,
> "His mercy endures forever."
> Let the house of Aaron say,
> "His mercy endures forever."
> Let those who fear the LORD say,
> "His mercy endures forever." (Ps 118:1-4)

This call includes everyone: the house of Israel, the house of Aaron (the priests), and those who fear the Lord (all believers). Then we begin to tell the story: "I called to the LORD in my distress; / he has answered and freed me" (118:5). We tell the whole story and then we form a procession. The priests in the temple hear us coming: "There are shouts of joy and salvation / in the tents of the just" (118:15). When we get to the sanctuary with the crowd we have gathered, we cry out:

"Open to me the gates of justice: / I will enter and thank the LORD" (118:19). The priests inside answer: "This is the LORD's own gate, / where the just enter" (118:20). In other words, "Do you know the password so we can let you in?"

The dialogue goes on, back and forth between the ministers on the inside and the crowd on the outside, and finally we are admitted to the sanctuary to have our celebration: "Blest is he who comes / in the name of the LORD. / We bless you from the house of the LORD" (118:26). We adorn the altar and then we pray—"You are my God, I praise you. / My God, I exalt you" (118:28)—and everyone joins in: "Give praise to the LORD, for he is good; / his mercy endures forever" (118:29).

We have come to the sanctuary to fulfill our vow, the promise we made when we were in trouble. Psalm 116 describes this offering:

> A thanksgiving sacrifice I make;
> I will call on the name of the LORD.
> My vows to the LORD I will fulfill
> before all his people,
> in the courts of the house of the LORD,
> in your midst, O Jerusalem.
>
> Alleluia! (Ps 116:17-19)

This gift of thanks (fulfilling our vow) is usually a sacrifice. The people of Israel had such a respect for the gift of life that they wouldn't think of killing an animal to eat it without first offering it to God, since the life belongs to God. To make a thanksgiving offering or communion sacrifice as it is described in Leviticus (7:11-21) and Deuteronomy (12:15-19), one slaughters the animal, offers a choice portion to God, and then—since the whole thing has to be eaten in a day (or at most two)—the whole family, the slaves, the Levites, and those from the highways and byways are brought in to share the banquet. No wonder the poor rejoice! It's probably the only time they get meat!

My vows I will pay before those who fear him.
The poor shall eat and shall have their fill.
They shall praise the LORD, those who seek him.
May their hearts live on forever and ever! (Ps 22:26b-27)

So the psalms teach us how to give thanks, how to become a thankful people. In the first moment of rescue, the "whew" moment, we turn to God with thanksgiving. Then we start to gather a crowd; we begin to tell the story of our terrible trouble. Then in a great procession we go to stand before God in the sanctuary to share our joy. We finish the story by bearing witness to God's wonderful goodness and then we have a party! (That's really what we're doing at Eucharist—which means "thanksgiving"! Don't forget it's a great party!) Think of the story of the prodigal son and all the other parables in Luke 15 (the lost sheep; the lost coin). They all end with a party! Actually, God is throwing the party because the treasure that was almost lost (us) has been found, has been rescued. The kingdom of heaven, after all, is a banquet—one great thanksgiving celebration where we'll all get to tell our stories and celebrate God's great love for us! And we'll never again get tired of the stories. Thanks be to God!

Exercise: Giving thanks

First, ponder these questions: What are the stories of deliverance that you have to tell? How have you shared in other's experience by actively listening to their stories? What are the wonders of God's love revealed to you for which you give thanks? Whom do you wish to gather to help you give thanks? Now write your own psalm of thanksgiving.

1. Begin with "I give you thanks, O Lord, because . . ."

2. Gather a crowd: summon all those who will help you give thanks (even if you summon them only in your imagination).

3. Then tell the story of the danger and distress: "I was in distress and God saved me; I was threatened and God delivered me." Don't be shy about describing your danger in detail!

4. Perhaps you may want to quote the lament you prayed when the danger threatened.

5. Renew the promises you made when you cried out in pain and lament.

Finally, make your thanksgiving offering to God and celebrate with a party!

Prayer: Gracious, compassionate God, you who wait for us with open arms. Accept our gift of thanks today for everything you give us—what we know and what we cannot even imagine. We make our prayer in Jesus' name, he who is always Yes! Amen.

Psalm 34:
Thanking God from A to Z

salm 34 is a thanksgiving psalm, but it has some special characteristics that belong to the wisdom tradition. The wisdom writers like order, so one of their techniques is to use the alphabet as a principle of organization. If you happen to be reading Psalm 34 in Hebrew, you will notice this use of the alphabet immediately. Each verse of the psalm begins with the next letter of the Hebrew alphabet (a poetic tour-de-force, to be sure). What can this ordering tell us about thanking God? What can we find in this very artificial structure to ponder? Actually, this psalm gives us everything, from A to Z, about our life with God. (If you're old enough, you'll remember the song "A, you're adorable; B, you're so beautiful; C, you're a cutie full of charm." Perhaps this is not the best example, but you get the idea. It's another attempt at completeness!) The psalmist is saying, "Do you want to know how good it is to live in God's presence? Do you want to know all the things we must be grateful for? I'll tell you, A to Z!"

Yet, in contrast to "A, you're adorable," this psalm is not all warm fuzzies. The psalm title (added later by some editor who wanted to help us get in the right mood to pray this psalm) gives us a historical note. This is a psalm "of David, when he pretended to be mad before Abimelech so that he drove him out and he went on his way." Actually, this ancient editor is wrong; the king is Achish (1 Sam 21:10-15). But the story is real. David, in fear for his life because he is being pursued by Saul, pretends to be mad, drooling and scratching on the doors of Achish's palace. Why does the poet set the tone for this psalm with this sobering story? Remember that the song of thanksgiving is still very close to the lament. We, like David, have just escaped a dangerous situation and still need to catch our breath. This little story reminds us that living surrounded by God's gifts doesn't mean there is a perfect world but that God is to be found in the midst of that all-too-messy history that we live in. The psalms are historical. The life they promise is in the very real world.

So what does the psalm say? Paradoxically, following that sobering title, the psalm begins, "I will bless the Lord at all times," in other words, "I will never stop thanking God" (ICEL). The whole first section (vv. 2-5) is a testimony of someone who has been answered by God, freed from all fears. This is the witness: "I sought the Lord, and he answered me; / from all my terrors he set me free" (v. 5). Over and over the psalmist returns to this theme, this wonder, that if we call, God hears; if we ask, God answers:

> This lowly one called; the Lord heard,
> and rescued him from all his distress.
>
> The Lord turns his eyes to the just,
> and his ears are open to their cry.
>
> When the just cry out, the Lord hears,
> and rescues them in all their distress. (Ps 34:7, 16, 18)

One message of Psalm 34 is certainly this: When we finally realize that whenever we call, God answers, there is no other response besides verse 2: "I will bless the LORD at all times!"

But not one of us knows how to celebrate this goodness of God alone. Can you have a party by yourself? When something good happens, we need friends to listen to the story and celebrate with us: "Glorify the LORD with me; together let us praise his name" (v. 4). The psalms are communal. They lead us to each other, to sing God's praise together.

The psalmist goes on (beginning in v. 6), mixing commands—turn to God, taste and see, come and listen to me (all invitations to others to join in giving praise)—with further descriptions of his own experience. Our lives, whether we want them to be or not, are both the Word of God to others and a call to praise.

At the midpoint of the psalm (vv. 9-12), we find the key: the heart of this psalm's teaching. This brief section begins and ends with familiar verses, such as, "Taste and see that the LORD is good," and, "Come, children, and hear me, / that I may teach you the fear of the LORD." Let us begin with fear of the Lord. What is "fear of the Lord"? Does it really mean that we should be afraid of God? Do we dread that God will judge us and condemn us? Absolutely not. It is, in fact, the opposite. The best definition I know came from a novice. She was assigned to give a report on "fear of the Lord," and she began by saying that it really means, "O, my God!" (Say it out loud with awe and you'll get the idea!) Fear of the Lord is everything that fills us with awe at God's goodness, everything that surprises us with the immensity of God's love for us. It is everything to which we respond, "O, my God!" It is that wonderful openness to life that children know. Fear of the Lord is the recognition that God is God and I am not—and I am glad! (Only in the last few years have I come to that last insight, and I think it is the heart of the matter—I am truly glad that God is God and I am not!) Fear of the Lord is the awe of love. This is what the psalmist is promising to teach us.

Fear of the Lord is introduced in Psalm 34 right after "taste and see": "Fear the Lord, you his holy ones. / They lack nothing, those who fear him" (v. 10). Here we find out *why* we might want to fear the Lord. We will want for nothing; we will lack nothing. This word translated "lack" or "want" is the same word we find in Psalm 23: "The Lord is my shepherd; / there is nothing I shall want" (Ps 23:1). There is absolutely nothing that we will lack if we fear God. The psalmist wants to be sure we get it, so the whole idea is repeated in verse 11: "The rich suffer want and go hungry, / but those who seek the Lord lack no blessing." If we fear the Lord we will lack nothing, nothing at all! This is pretty good motivation for the next verse: "Come, children, and hear me, / that I may teach you the fear of the Lord" (Ps 34:12). By now we should be begging to learn fear of the Lord!

Keeping in mind that fear of the Lord means we will lack nothing good, I would like to return to verse 9, the first verse of this little cluster: "Taste and see that the Lord is good" (34:9). The goodness we will not lack is the very goodness of God: "One does not live by bread alone, but by every word that comes from the mouth of the Lord" (Deut 8:3). God nourishes us in only one way: by being present within us. The word translated "taste" has the deeper meaning of to "savor" or "discern." It's richer than just tasting the spaghetti for dinner; instead, this is the word for the connoisseur of fine wine. The ICEL translation says, "Drink in the richness of God." NAB (1991) said, "Learn to savor how good the Lord is."[1] We are fed by God through every experience of our lives; the word of God comes to us in the Scripture which bathes us daily, in our families and communities, all those with whom we live. We are fed by everything we experience: what we feel and hear and taste and see. Daily, weekly, we hear: "Take, eat; this is my body. . . . Drink . . . for this is my blood of the covenant, which is poured out for many for the forgiveness of sins" (Matt 26:26-28). Daily we are nourished by God's word proclaimed in our liturgy. We live now, not we, but Christ in us. Do you long for life? Drink in the richness of God. Do you desire to see good days? Learn to savor the Lord. Those who seek God lack no good thing!

To share food is to share life. Christ lives not only in me but in all of us together. We are bound to those with whom we eat because our lives have been joined together. Eating the same food has made us one body, one flesh. And so the psalmist's following words of wisdom are vitally important:

> Guard your tongue from evil,
> and your lips from speaking deceit.
> Turn aside from evil and do good.
> Seek after peace, and pursue it. (Ps 34:14-15)

If we are one body, how can we afford to let our tongues run to evil, our lips to speak lies? If we are one body, how can we afford not to seek after peace? As one body, it will not be enough for us simply to turn from evil, we must actively seek to do good for one another wherever we have the chance. After all, it is our own lives we are nourishing. As St. Benedict exhorts his followers at the end of his Rule, we will be eager to try to be the first to show respect to one another, supporting with the greatest patience one another's weaknesses of body or behavior. Our only competition will be competition in obedience to one another, as we pursue not so much what is good for ourselves but what is good for each other (RB 72.4–7). We are one body. We respond, "I do," to the question, "Who is it who desires life?" and the life we find is one life. Here again, we cannot escape each other! St. Benedict teaches us to pray that even in heaven we may be with each other: "Prefer nothing whatever to Christ, and may he bring us *all together* to everlasting life!" (RB 72.11–12, my emphasis).

The end of Psalm 34 (vv. 16-23) simply draws out the consequences of our choice. If you would be happy, there are two ways lying before you. Those who turn to evil are confronted by God and destroyed by the evil they choose. Those who fear the Lord are delighted by the presence of God, the goodness of the Lord. They call out; God hears. God heals their broken hearts, watches over all their bones. (Psalm prayer has to do with bodies, after all!) Who is there who longs for life and desires to see good days? "Look toward [God] and be radiant; / let your faces not be abashed" (Ps 34:6).

So what words does this A-to-Z psalm give us to murmur for the rest of the day? I have four (or perhaps five). You can take your choice or choose them all. First of all, we ponder the central question of this psalm: "do you long for life?" I'm deep enough into middle age to know that this is a real question. David is a good example for us. He certainly longed for life and took hold of it with both hands. He may not always have been prudent, but he certainly cannot be accused of not having lived. Do you long for life? Are you willing to find it in the world you live in? Are you willing to share it with the others who live with you and around you?

Second, the beginning of the psalm gives us two wonderful sentences to murmur: "I will bless the Lord at all times." This is certainly a recipe for happiness. The most grateful people are, without a doubt, the happiest. And "glorify the Lord with me." This is a recipe for life with others. It is diametrically opposed to murmuring. But the superscription that tells the story of David (v. 1) keeps these two sentences from being the over-zealous, mealy-mouthed, pious piffle which makes us all a little nauseous. It is in the honesty of everyday life that we learn to say truly, "I will bless the Lord at all times; glorify the Lord with me." It is from each other—from the courage of those who suffer, from the faith of those who are dying, from the perseverance of those who just keep showing up to do good to others every day—that we learn to murmur these words. This is our gift of life.

Third, be awed at God's goodness; "fear the Lord." How can we learn what we knew as children, to be overcome by wonder at the goodness of God? This is radical openness; this is true vulnerability. This is the gift of waking up every day and thanking God that the sun came up again and I am still alive, still in awe at God's great love for me. I lack no good thing.

Finally, "taste and see that the LORD is good" or "drink in the richness of God," or "learn to savor how good the Lord is." We are what we eat. It is the life of God within us that makes us happy, that is our true life. Taste and see how good it is! It is the life of God within us that makes us one body. (That scares us a little, I think. At least it scares me when I think about it!) There is an old folktale told about a monastic community that was dying until a Rabbi told them, "One of you is the Messiah." As the monks lived day by day looking for the face of Christ in each of their brother monks, the monastery gradually began to flourish. It came to life. We are what we eat. If you would be happy, taste the goodness of the Lord living within you. Savor the goodness of the Lord living within everyone you meet. Even if powerful people go hungry, those seeking God lack no good thing.

In his Rule, St. Benedict quotes the central question of this psalm as the initial invitation to his followers: "Is there anyone here who yearns for life and desires to see good days" (RB Prol. 15). What can we say except, "I do!" Then God promises us:

> If you desire true and eternal life, keep your tongue free from vicious talk and your lips from all deceit; turn away from evil and do good; let peace be your quest and aim. Once you have done this, my eyes will be upon you and my ears will listen for your prayers; and even before you ask me, I will say to you: Here I am (Isa 58:9). What, dear friends, is more delightful than this voice of the Lord calling to us?" (RB Prol. 16–19)

What, indeed, could be more delightful! Our thanksgiving always returns to the true source of our joy: the presence of God.

Exercise: Take some time to list from A to Z what you are thankful for. Use the alphabet as your guide: "I thank you God for apples and anniversaries; I thank you for bees and bananas and birthdays." Have fun!

Prayer: God of all seasons, of our youth, our middle age, and our golden years, nourish us every day by the delights of your presence and the bread of your Word. Then we will never stop thanking you. This we ask in the name of Jesus your son, Emmanuel, God with us. Amen.

Trusting God

rust is a very fragile commodity in our time. Perhaps it always was. Think about this. Whom do you trust? Your family? Your president? Your pastor? Your friends? The media? There have been too many betrayals of trust in recent memory for us to give it easily. Too many people have broken faith. We have seen government leaders lie and religious leaders prey on the vulnerable. We are bombarded with advertising that promises things we know the product cannot deliver. In politics we hear plenty of promises that we doubt will be fulfilled. Yet there *are* people and groups who are quite worthy of trust. How do we learn to trust? How do we know when and how to trust? How do we learn to trust God and to trust each other? How do we learn to be trustworthy ourselves?

First I want to look at the psalms, and then I want to ponder some contemporary examples. The psalms of confidence, like the psalms of thanksgiving, develop the final section of the lament but are distinguished from the lament by emphasis. The focus of the lament is the distress of the sufferer, while the focus of the psalm of confidence is that God can and will protect us.

We have moved a step beyond the psalms of thanksgiving, and, as a result, we aren't quite as fragile. God has saved us often enough to give us hope that God will do it again. We are aware of danger, but we cannot be shaken—even if an army should stand against us (Ps 27:3). We know whom we trust: "In God alone be at rest, my soul" (Ps 62:6). We are sure God hears us, loves us, is powerful enough to save us. We can declare to those who threaten us, "In the LORD I have taken refuge" (Ps 11:1). The tone is often quiet and gentle: "Truly, I have set my soul / in tranquility and silence" (Ps 131:2). We know that if we keep hold of God we cannot be shaken (Ps 16:8). We rest as secure as a child on its mother's lap (Ps 131).

Psalm 27 gives us a sense of the conflicting emotions that run through the psalms of confidence. We begin:

> The LORD is my light and my salvation;
> whom shall I fear?
> The LORD is the stronghold of my life;
> whom should I dread? (Ps 27:1)

What do you think? Is this person afraid? The statement is very strong, but when do you use these verses? When you're on top of the world? Or when you are terrified? Is this a little like whistling in the dark? We are not quite as close to the danger as we were in the psalms of thanksgiving, but we still know the thrill of danger, which might be around the next corner—even in the next verse!

> When those who do evil draw near
> to devour my flesh,
> it is they, my enemies and foes,
> who stumble and fall. (Ps 27:2)

Now we list those who, indeed, might make us afraid! A violent mob, an army, surrounding warfare. Should we understand these literally? Probably not. Still, there are all too many people for whom this is a daily reality, for example, Iraqis, Afghans, Pakistanis, Syrians, Israelis, Palestinians. But these psalms are for us too. If we are honest, we are forced to admit that sometimes we too are afraid or disillusioned. The psalmist is giving us words for that fear that nibbles at the corners of our life or stands like a giant in the door. The psalmist is also giving us words to declare our trust in God even when we do not feel like trusting anyone.

As Psalm 27 continues, we realize that the very form of this psalm teaches us the basis for our trust.[1] The psalmist has constructed his poem in a concentric pattern, meaning that the beginning and the end are similar. The verses just inside the beginning and the end are also similar. The psalm continues moving from both ends toward the center, where the main point is. Simply, the structure looks like this:

A Expression of firm confidence, even though danger lurks (v. 1)

   B The enemy threatens (vv. 2-3)

      C What is most important to us is God's presence (vv. 4-10)

   B' The enemy threatens (vv. 11-12)

A' Expression of firm confidence and encouragement of others (vv. 13-14)

If we look more closely at the psalm, we see how this structure works. The strong confidence we expressed in verse 1 comes back at the end in verses 13-14:

> I believe I shall see the LORD's goodness
> in the land of the living.
> Wait for the LORD; be strong;
> be stouthearted, and wait for the LORD!

The enemies who appeared right after the beginning in verses 2-3 reappear right before the end:

> Instruct me, Lord, in your way;
> on an even path lead me
> because of my enemies.
> Do not leave me to the will of my foes,
> for false witnesses rise up against me,
> and they breathe out violence. (Ps 27:11-12)

So we move toward the center and plead for what we really want: to see God's face. To see God's face is enough for us; this is our longing and the reason for our trust (verses 4, 7-10):

> There is one thing I ask of the Lord,
> only this do I seek:
> to live in the house of the Lord
> all the days of my life,
> to gaze on the beauty of the Lord,
> to inquire at his temple. (Ps 27:4)
>
> O Lord, hear my voice when I call;
> have mercy and answer me.
> Of you my heart has spoken,
> "Seek his face."
>
> It is your face, O Lord, that I seek;
> hide not your face from me.
> Dismiss not your servant in anger;
> you have been my help.
>
> Do not abandon or forsake me,
> O God, my Savior!
> Though father and mother forsake me,
> the Lord will receive me. (Ps 27:7-10)

The very center of the psalm reassures us that our trust is not misplaced (verses 5-6):

For there he keeps me safe in his shelter
in the day of evil.
He hides me under cover of his tent;
he sets me high upon a rock.
And now my head shall be raised
above my foes who surround me,
and I shall offer within his tent
a sacrifice of joy.
I will sing and make music for the Lord. (Ps 27:5-6)

All we want is God. God's presence at the center of the psalm and in the very center of our hearts is the power that conquers our fear.

Throughout this psalm we have been speaking first to God and then to the community. God is named fourteen times in this psalm of fourteen verses. Thirteen times we call on God by the sacred name "Yahweh" (indicated in English by using small capital letters in the word "Lord") and once simply as "God, my Savior." We may have a heightened awareness of all the danger that is around us—adrenaline is a wonderful thing—but, no matter what, we're not letting go of God. In Psalm 23 we declare the same reason for confidence: "Though I should walk in the valley of the shadow of death, / no evil would I fear, for you are with me" (Ps 23:4). In Psalm 62 we say, "In God alone is my soul at rest; / my salvation comes from him" (Ps 62:2). We seek God's face; we long to live in God's house. The enemy can get in under our confidence but cannot touch what is at the center, our hope in God's presence. That is the source of our trust. Nothing else matters.

My favorite psalm of confidence is not in the Psalter; it is the canticle of Habakkuk. Habakkuk is called to prophesy at a time of great crisis in Judah. Babylon is gaining dominance over the whole ancient Near East. They have defeated the Egyptians and driven them back to the south. They have taken Judah's leaders and prominent people into exile. The prophet fears even greater disaster because of the corruption in Judah. He is right! Under Nebuchadnezzar the Babylonians will destroy Jerusalem and take many more of its people into exile (587 BCE). But even as he suffers terror that makes his stomach churn and his knees buckle, he has the courage to pray:

> Though the fig tree does not blossom,
> and no fruit is on the vines;
> though the produce of the olive fails,
> and the fields yield no food;
> though the flock is cut off from the fold,
> and there is no herd in the stalls,
> yet I will rejoice in the Lord;
> I will exult in the God of my salvation. (Hab 3:17-18)

We have other examples of trust in God. Job says, "Slay me though he might, I will wait for him" (Job 13:15; NABRE). At age seventy-five, Abraham packs up and sets out to go to the land God will show him—without a map, without directions (Gen 12:4). When descendants don't come, he complains to God, but at God's reassurance he believes—even without evidence (Gen 15:2-5). This faith in God's promise is his righteousness (Gen 15:6). Sarah too was called to trust. She too had to leave everything familiar and set out on a journey to an unknown place. Abraham, at least, had heard the voice of God. Sarah is much more like us. She had to trust someone else to hear the voice of God: Abraham, in his vision. We too must often discern the voice of God in the voice of another person.

Our primary examples of trusting obedience to God are Mary, who, with very little information, declares, "Behold, I am the handmaid of the Lord. May it be done to me according to your word" (Luke 1:38), and Mary's son, who, in agony, can still say to his Father, "Not my will but yours be done" (Luke 22:42).

Saint Augustine points out that this radical trust in God is only possible to those who are humble, who know that they are dependent on God for everything. If we rely on our own strength, we will certainly fall. We will certainly be defeated. We are neither powerful enough nor wise enough to escape all the evils that threaten us. "In God alone is my soul at rest" (Ps 62:2). Or as Psalm 121 says:

> The LORD will guard you from evil;
> he will guard your soul.
> The LORD will guard your going and coming,
> both now and forever. (Ps 121:7-8)

Commenting on this verse of Psalm 121, Augustine says:

> Guard yourselves, but not by any strength of your own, for the Lord is your defense and your guardian, the Lord who neither grows drowsy nor sleeps. Once only did he sleep for us; but he rose again, and now he will never sleep any more.[2]

We have contemporary examples of this undying trust in God also. A few years ago I read the story of the seven Trappist monks who were kidnapped and killed in Algeria in 1996.[3] You may have seen the film *Of Gods and Men*, which also tells their story. These brave monks remained in their monastery out of faithfulness to their little village community, even as the violence spread all around them. They knew death could come at any moment. Some of their letters express the mixture of emotion found in the psalms of confidence. For example,

> *This is from Brother Luc, a physician:*
> We are now "at risk," but our community stays on. Fear is the lack of faith. We follow the path of our Lord. He shows us the way—it is one of poverty, failure, and death. . . . Meanwhile, I will do my work, receive the poor and the sick, awaiting the

day when I will close my eyes to enter into God's house, whose door is open to all who knock. . . .

Pray for me, my dear friend, that my departure from this world be in the Peace and Joy of Jesus.[4]

This is from Brother Paul to his father, after eight religious men and women had been killed:

Dear Father,

No one has any illusions anymore. Each of us knows that tomorrow could be his turn. But each of us has freely chosen to stay. . . . The terrorist group that rules our sector has obviously judged us, as yet, not sufficiently interesting to bother with. But if *raison d'état* requires, other groups can put pressure on our local emir to pluck us away, since we offer such an easy and choice prize to whoever wants us.[5]

From Brother Christian, the prior:

If the day comes, and it could be today, that I am a victim of the terrorism that seems to be engulfing all foreigners living in Algeria, I would like my community, my Church, and my family to remember that I have dedicated my life to God and Algeria.

If the moment comes, I would hope to have the presence of mind, and the time, to ask for God's pardon and for that of my fellowman, and, at the same time, to pardon in all sincerity he who would attack me.[6]

This is radical trust in God.

Most of us are not called to such extreme trust and confidence. Or are we? Daily faithfulness to God is an ongoing surrender of our lives. The daily embrace of whatever life brings is an expression of radical trust in God. The daily gift of whatever energy and resources we have to cheer and comfort others is a minute-by-minute witness to our confidence in God. Saint Benedict places his exhortation to trust in a position of emphasis, the very last of the Tools of Good Works: "Never lose hope in God's mercy" (RB 4.74).[7]

I have a homey example of what this undying day-after-day trust and hope looks like. Our Sister Helena, who died in December 2006 at the age of ninety-seven, was the last of our German-born sisters. She came to the community when she was twenty years old. She taught in grade schools throughout the Midwest for forty some years and then came home to Atchison where, as her obituary says, "she assisted in various services and was an example of someone who had learned to 'pray always.'" For me she was an example of total confidence in God. During the last years of her life she was always at St. Lucy chapel in our infirmary wing. But she wasn't a plaster saint. She knew how to be in God's presence with all her human quirks. One of these was her love of sweets. She could often be seen kneeling before the Blessed Sacrament eating Oreo cookies. When the carpet was replaced in that chapel, the workers found lots of candy wrappers stuffed down the hole where a heating pipe came up.

But the final example of her trust came as she approached death. The head nurse and the director of Dooley Center were in her room deciding that the time had come for us to sit with her. Sister Helena perked up and said, "Am I going to die?" They replied in the affirmative, and from that time on whenever anyone of us passed her room, she waved at us. She kissed the hand of those who sat with her. She was telling us goodbye. But she also waved up at the corner of her room with great delight. What did she see? I don't know, but I think her two blood sisters, who were also in our community and had gone off to heaven ahead of her, were leaning over heaven's gate and telling her to hurry up! I will never experience a better example of a happy death. This is the confidence we aspire to.

The psalms of confidence are an honest acknowledgment of our very real terrors and our gritty, gutsy trust in God despite our fear. We are called to testify that, no matter how perilous our world may be, we will never abandon our confidence in God. We are not left to bear this testimony alone, however. We are surrounded by a cloud of witnesses from Abraham to these twentieth-century monks to our own Sister

Helenas, all of whom declare that God is indeed trustworthy. They testify with their blood (remember, "martyr" means "witness") that they never stopped trusting God, never stopped seeking God's face—even in the faces of their killers. They testify with their daily, courageous acceptance of whatever life brings. They give flesh to these psalms that had soaked into their bones as they soak into ours. They help us declare, in the words of Psalm 125:

> Those who put their trust in the LORD
> are like Mount Sion, that cannot be shaken,
> that stands forever. (Ps 125:1)

In the First Letter of Peter, we are urged: "Always be ready to make your defense to anyone who demands from you an accounting for the hope that is in you; yet do it with gentleness and reverence" (1 Pet 3:15-16; NRSV). Always be ready. God will never abandon us.

In whom do you trust? What or who has led you to trust in God? What shakes your trust? How do you help others to trust?

Exercise: Search your memory for a time you were in danger or were despondent. Consider how God drew you out of that miry pit or saved you from that danger. Recognize how trustworthy God is. Then write your own psalm of trust. Perhaps you might want to imitate the psalmist of Psalm 27 and put your most important insight at the center of your psalm.

Prayer: Ever-faithful God, you surround us with your loving care, we trust in you. Help us when our trust is shaken. We make our prayer in Jesus' name, he who shows us the wonder of your trust in us. Amen.

The 90s: God Is King

There is a special collection of psalms in the fourth book of the Psalter that not only declares God is king, but gives us words to proclaim how glad we are that this is true. The psalms from 93 to 100—with the possible exception of Psalm 94—belong to this group. One of the newer approaches to analyzing the psalms is to consider their context by looking at the order in which we find them. What does it mean to pray Psalm 23, "The Lord is my shepherd" (Ps 23:1), right after Psalm 22, "My God, my God, why have you forsaken me?" (Ps 22:2). Or how do we read Psalm 51, "My sacrifice to God, a broken spirit: / a broken and humbled heart" (Ps 51:19), after Psalm 50:

> I do not take more bullocks from your farms,
> nor goats from among your herds.
> Were I hungry, I would not tell you,
> for the world and its fullness is mine. (Ps 50:9, 12)

So looking at Psalms 93–100 together will give us insight into each of these individual psalms.

These psalms were most likely sung around Sukkoth, the fall harvest festival, and celebrate the fact that God will rule over the people for another year. All of these psalms reflect the weather in Israel during the fall interchange period. (Did you ever think to look for weather patterns in the psalms? Does the weather reveal God to you?) This interchange between the summer dry season and the winter rainy season is a very stormy period. Sometimes the wind blows from the east; a hot wind off the Arabian desert that brings dust storms and the burning sirocco, or as the people of the Near East call it, the *khamsin*. (The Santa Ana winds in California are another example of this weather phenomenon.) Sometimes the wind blows from the west, a wet wind off of the Mediterranean, bringing powerful rain storms. Sometimes it seems the two winds are fighting.

Psalm 93 shows us the wet west wind. We are assured that God's throne stands firm and will not be moved, no matter how violent the storm. Even if the flood rises and roars and the waves pound against the shore, God is still in charge (Ps 93:2-3).

> Greater than the roar of mighty waters,
> more glorious than the surgings of the sea,
> the LORD is glorious on high. (Ps 93:4)

Psalm 95, dear to all who pray the Liturgy of the Hours as the invitatory psalm, reminds us that God's hands hold the depths of the earth, the tops of the mountains, the sea and the dry land. God formed them by hand and they belong to God (Ps 95:3-4). We are warned not to harden our hearts as the Israelites did at Meribah and Massah when they doubted that God could give them water (Ps 95:8-9). The hot desert wind must be making us fretful and rebellious.

Psalms 96 and 98 echo each other at the end. We can almost hear the rain:

> Let the heavens rejoice and earth be glad;
> let the sea and all within it thunder praise.
> Let the land and all it bears rejoice.
> Then will all the trees of the wood shout for joy.
> (Ps 96:11-12)

Why is all creation rejoicing? Because it is raining! What do trees sound like in the rain? Listen to the bodies of water. Can you hear the sea thunder? Listen to the joy of the thirsty earth. What does this mean? The Lord is coming to rule the earth with justice and truth. Our creator is providing water that will provide everything else that we need. The rains have come. I've seen pictures of farmers during the dust bowl who dashed out of the house when the first raindrops fell and simply danced in the storm. That is what is happening at the end of Psalm 96. Psalm 98 reports almost the same experience.

> Let the sea and all within it thunder;
> the world, and those who dwell in it.
> Let the rivers clap their hands,
> and the hills ring out their joy. (Ps 98:7-8)

Listen to raindrops on water. Can you hear the rivers clap their hands? The hills shout with them for joy. It's raining! Shout for joy before the Lord who comes in the storm, the Lord who cares for every living thing. We will have a new growing season; we will not starve. God has once more given the rain.

Psalms 97 and 99 are east wind psalms. In Psalm 97 we hear thunder and see heat lightning (lightning when there is no rain). God is surrounded by a dark cloud. The mighty mountains seem to melt like soft wax at the arrival of the Lord. God's enemies are destroyed, blown away like chaff in the hot dry wind. But God's faithful walk in light and joy. God reigns over all. We rejoice and sing.

In Psalm 99 both the people and the earth tremble at the news that "the LORD is king" (Ps 99:1). The just ones whom we met in Psalm 97 are led by Old Testament heroes: Aaron, Moses, Samuel. The dust cloud of the sirocco (Ps 97) is now seen as the pillar of cloud that followed Israel during the exodus sojourn and from which God speaks. The refrain reminds us that "the LORD our God is holy" (Ps 99:9; cf. 97:3, 5).

Psalm 100 closes this collection. It is the thanksgiving hymn when the battle of the winds is over and we are all at home in the new Jerusalem: enter God's presence with joy; God's love is forever. (This psalm will be treated in greater detail in the last chapter.)

What can we learn from this collection of psalms? We begin in Psalm 96 with the command, "O sing a new song to the LORD" (Ps 96:1). The command is repeated at the beginning of Psalm 98. What can that mean? If we keep singing these psalms, how can the song be new? What is new about the song that we and the whole earth are supposed to sing again and again? The psalms go on to tell us: It is God's salvation— every day (Ps 96:2; 98:1-2)! Day after day! God has revealed this salvation to us and delivered us from our enemies (Ps 98:2). The psalmist tells us the wonderful news: "God has remembered his merciful love" (Ps 98:3). God's love is fresh every day, "eternal his merciful love" (Ps 100:5). The song has to be new because the salvation is new; the love is everlasting. We are called by these psalms to announce the good news everywhere: God's salvation (the Hebrew word here is *yeshua*, which is Jesus' name in Hebrew), God's glory, God's wonderful acts, God's undying love. Saint Augustine says:

> The new song your heart is singing reaches the ears of God who made you a new person. You love, and you are silent, but your love is itself a voice that sings to God; your love itself is the new song. Do you want proof of this? The Lord tells us, *A new commandment I give you: that you love one another* (Jn 13:34).[1]

The psalms in this collection cannot quit giving us imperatives: sing, proclaim, shout, tell, give God glory, worship, tremble, bow down, rejoice. But after all these commands, we come to the real point: "Say to the nations: 'The LORD is king'" (Ps 96:10). What does it mean that God is king? Why are we so overjoyed by this? Why is all creation thrilled at this news? To understand this we need to back up and take a broader look at the context. In fact, the whole Psalter is shaped by the conviction that we sing for joy because God is king. Now if the Psalter is shaped by this assertion, then our prayer is also. So it is essential to grasp the proclamation these psalms are making.

In the first two books of the Psalter (Pss 1–72), the Davidic king is very prominent. Book 2 ends with Psalm 72, where the king is the best possible thing that could have happened. Wherever he is, the nourishing rain falls; where he walks, the crops grow (Ps 72:6, 16). His presence is a blessing; he establishes justice for the poor and peace for all people (Ps 72:3-4, 12-14). It doesn't get better than this. But in book 3 (Pss 73–89), everything falls apart. We have psalms that talk about the invasion of enemies (Pss 74 and 83). Psalm 79 describes in gruesome detail the destruction of the temple. The wicked seem to prosper (Ps 73) and the faithful are left in darkness (Ps 88). Book 3 ends with Psalm 89.

> But yet you have spurned and rejected,
> you are angry with the one you have anointed.
> You have renounced your covenant with your servant,
> and dishonored his crown in the dust.
>
> You have brought his glory to an end;
> you have hurled his throne to the ground.
>
> Where are your mercies of the past, O Lord,
> which you swore in your faithfulness to David?
>
> (Ps 89:39-40, 45, 50)

It can't get much worse. The Davidic king, God's "anointed" (i.e., "messiah"), has been defeated and humiliated. Where are God's promises now?

Book 4 (Pss 90–106) gives us the joyful answer. Here we have this whole series of glorious psalms we have just considered, psalms that announce in no uncertain terms that *God is king!* The earthly kingship was nice while it lasted, but in the end it failed. Now we depend on God alone. So Psalms 93–100 call us to announce that "The LORD is king!"

In his book, *The Lord's Song in a Foreign Land*, Thomas Wahl observes that this announcement can be quite subversive.[2] What if God really is king? What if we acted on this announcement? What would the world be like? Who would rejoice? For whom would this be good news? Will this "new song" be received by everyone with delight? Maybe not! Psalm 97 talks about the enemies of God being consumed in blazing fire (Ps 97:3). But for those who serve God and hope in God's name, this is the best news. The Lord is coming. The heavens and the earth, the sea and the plains are all glad. All creation rejoices if God is in charge. They are delighted when God comes. We are commissioned to announce to everyone, "The Lord is king." We must sing the new song, and sing and sing and sing. How will we know the song? Augustine reminds us that the new song is love: God's love for us and our love of God and one another.

The unbelievable love of God for us is shown in the three Masses of Christmas and, appropriately, Psalms 96, 97, and 98 are the responsorial psalms chosen for these three celebrations of the Eucharist.[3] We may be surprised that three psalms declaring God's kingship are chosen for this feast. We sit in church enjoying the fragrance of the evergreens, listening to Christmas carols, and feeling tender as we look at the baby in the crib. We may even be moved by the procession of a small child carrying the infant Christ to the manger. How then can we sing this powerful song: "The LORD is king"? Wouldn't we be more comfortable singing a refrain such as,

"The Lord is tender and caring"? Perhaps. But there are no more fitting responses for Christmas than these kingship psalms.

This newborn baby is indeed the Lord—the king of the whole earth. At midnight we hear the coronation song given to us by the prophet Isaiah (9:1-6). This child is called "Wonderful Counselor, Mighty God, Everlasting Father, Prince of Peace" (Isa 9:6). He will sit on David's throne and rule over his kingdom forever. This is the "good news of great joy" that the angels announce to the shepherds and to us. We must sing the new song, Psalm 96; we must proclaim this news to the whole world! In the morning we sing Psalm 98, the companion to Psalm 96. Now in the light that no darkness can quench, "all the ends of the earth have seen / the salvation of our God" (Ps 98:3; see John 1:4-5). God, out of love, has taken on our human nature. This use of the psalms in the liturgies tells us what it means that God is king. It is indeed subversive. As St. Irenaeus says, "He became what we are that we might become what he is."[4]

The most surprising use, however, is in the Mass at Dawn. Psalm 97 is an east wind psalm with fire, lightning, and a trembling earth. The terror of God's power in the psalm is juxtaposed with the story of humble people awed by God's great love. In the gospel (Luke 2:15-20) we meet the shepherds going to Bethlehem in joyful awe, even as we sing "the mountains melt like wax / before the face of the LORD" (Ps 97:5). They find the child lying in a manger as we sing, "The skies proclaim his justice; / all peoples see his glory" (Ps 97:6). Mary treasures their words and the shepherds go home, "glorifying and praising God for all they had heard and seen" (Luke 2:20). We acclaim:

> Light shines forth for the just one,
> and joy for the upright of heart.
> Rejoice in the LORD, you just;
> to the memory of his holiness give thanks. (Ps 97:11-12)

The message given to us by these psalms is that God is, indeed, the all-powerful king over the whole earth. But our almighty God has "emptied himself, / taking the form of a slave, / being born in human likeness" (Phil 2:7). God has taken on the whole of our human nature—all of our glory and all of our weakness (except sin)—in order to teach us how to be truly who we are. This is what the kingship of God means. This is what God's rule over us brings. This is the good news!

Exercise: Listen to today's news. Where do you see the hidden rule of God? What can you do to make others aware of God's generous rule?

Prayer: All-powerful God, you who created both the gentle breeze and the overwhelming gale, teach us to find you in every wind that blows. Protect us from all that would harm us and refresh us with your presence. This we ask in the name of Jesus, who promised us your Spirit. Amen.

Praising God

We have been given a great gift in the psalms. It is our privilege to pray them frequently, even daily, to let them soak into our bones over a lifetime. They teach us how to tell the story of God's love in our lives, how to cry out our pain without abandoning hope, how to sing unending praise to God. As Pope John Paul II said, "the Book of Psalms remains the ideal source of Christian prayer."[1] This rhythm of the psalms is our lifeblood.

We have taken the time to tell our story and cry out our pain. We have given thanks and declared our unfailing trust in God. Now we move to praise, to doxology. The Psalter itself—after the introductory Psalms 1–2—moves from lament to praise. The greatest number of laments is in the first half of the Psalter; the greatest number of hymns in the second. This movement is not continuous, but it is constant. Another hint to the direction of the Psalter is this: two important phrases also occur in the last third of the Psalter: "God's love endures forever" and "Hallelujah!" The structure of the Psalter gives us a pattern for our lives.

In the hymns we stand in awe of God who created the whole universe and yet uses that almighty power to care for the vulnerable. The hymns are disinterested praise. Where the former psalms are focused on ourselves—our story, our danger, our rescue, what God has done for *us*—the hymns are focused entirely on God. This is where we really do make God the subject of every verb.

Just as the laments had something to teach us about how to cry out our pain, the hymns teach us how to give praise. They are much simpler than the laments. Our lives are much less complex when we move to praise than they are in the thick of the lament. Hymns have only two parts: a call to praise and the reasons for praise. Sometimes, the call to praise returns at the end.

The call to praise, in contrast to the cry of the lament, is not addressed to God. Instead we call out to everyone and everything we can think of to help us praise our great and powerful God. None of us is really capable alone of praising the awesome goodness of God. So first we summon up our own strength: "Bless the LORD, O my soul" (Ps 103:1); "My soul, give praise to the LORD; / I will praise the LORD all my life" (Ps 146:1b-2a). Then we call all believers, "Sing a new song to the LORD. . . . Let Israel rejoice in its Maker" (Ps 149:1a, 2a); "Come, let us ring out our joy to the LORD; / hail the rock who saves us" (Ps 95:1). We call all nations: "O praise the LORD, all you nations; / acclaim him, all you peoples!" (Ps 117:1). We call all creation: "Cry out with joy to the LORD, all the earth" (Ps 100:1). We even call all the angels, all heavenly beings: "Ascribe to the LORD, you heavenly powers, / ascribe to the LORD glory and strength" (Ps 29:1).

The most complete call to praise is in Psalm 148:

> Praise the Lord!
> Across the heavens,
> From the heights,

all you angels, heavenly beings,
sing praise, sing praise!

Sun and moon, glittering stars,
sing praise, sing praise.
Highest heavens, rain clouds,
sing praise, sing praise.

Praise God's name,
whose word called you forth
and fixed you in place for ever
by eternal decree.

Let there be praise:
from depths of the earth,
from creatures of the deep.

Fire and hail, snow and mist,
storms, winds,
mountains, hills,
fruit trees and cedars,
wild beasts and tame,
snakes and birds,

princes, judges,
rulers, subjects,
men, women,
old and young,
praise, praise the holy name,
this name beyond all names. (Ps 148:1-13)[2]

The call to praise always implies community. We are in this together. In the call to praise we take up our responsibility for the rest of creation, given to us in Genesis: "have dominion over the fish of the sea and over the birds of the air and over every living thing that moves upon the earth" (Gen 1:28). We take up our responsibility to be the bridge between the rest of creation and God, we who are made of the clay of the earth and breathe with the breath of God (Gen 2:7). We take up our responsibility to be the lungs for the earth. If we cut ourselves off from God, God's life-giving breath, the whole earth suffocates. The prophets tell us that over and over:

> How long will the land mourn,
> and the grass of every field wither?
> For the wickedness of those who live in it
> the animals and the birds are swept away. (Jer 12:4)

Part of our responsibility is to bring all creation to praise God with us. So we call to all creation to praise God.

We summon all people, all creation, because we are so aware that alone we could never give enough praise to God. We are simply too inadequate, too puny. As a result, we gather reinforcements. In the turn to hope at the end of Psalm 22, we even call those who are dead and the people yet unborn to join in our praise of God (Ps 22:30-32).

After we call everyone to help us give praise, we begin to tell the reasons for praising our God. Every good thing we experience is a reason to praise God. The heavens, "the work of . . . [God's] fingers," amaze us (Ps 8:4). God made them by a word (Ps 33:6) and they, in turn, "declare the glory of God" (Ps 19:2). God sends the sun rejoicing on its daily round (Ps 19:6-7). God "made the moon to mark the months" and, with the stars, to rule the night (Ps 104:19; 136:8). All time is in God's hands. God made the animals and gives them water and food (Ps 104:10-11, 14). All creation sings with delight at God's justice: the trees "shout for joy," the sea thunders, the "rivers clap their hands," and "the hills ring out their joy" (Ps 96:11-13; 98:7-9). Most of all, however, we praise God for all the gifts to us. God made us, shepherds us, loves us (Ps 100:3, 5). God feeds us and guards us (Ps 145:15-16, 20). God reveals the word of salvation to us (Ps 147:19). But God does have favorites! Our God uses divine power most often for the poor and needy, each one. We call everyone to praise God who hears the cry of the poor (Ps 34:18), who sustains the widow and orphan (Ps 146:9), who feeds the hungry (Ps 145:15-16), who gives sight to the blind (Ps 146:8), who never forgets the needy (Ps 113:7).

These reasons for praise are usually introduced with the little Hebrew word *"ki,"* which we usually translate as "for" or "because." For example, "Praise the Lord, because the Lord is faithful." But *ki* can often be understood as "indeed" or "wow!" "Praise the Lord for God is loving," can be "Praise the Lord, indeed/wow, God is loving!" This little word *ki* is the word used in Genesis 1 when God looks at everything that has been created and says *ki tob* (Gen 1:4, 10, 12, 18, 21, 25)—"wow! That's good!" In Psalm 100 we return the compliment. Our reason for giving praise is the simplest there is: "Indeed how good is the LORD, / eternal his merciful love" (Ps 100:5). Try that sometime with a psalm. Instead of saying, "Give thanks to the Lord, for God is good," say, "Give thanks to the Lord! Wow, God is good!" (Not in public prayer, of course!)

The reasons for praising God are often expressed with participles—the "–ing" form of the verb. That sets these reasons in the continuing present.

For example, in Psalm 103:3-5 (my translation):

> God is forgiving all your guilt,
> healing every one of your ills,
> redeeming your life from the grave,
> crowning you with love and compassion,
> filling your life with good things,
> your youth is renewed like an eagle's.

All of this is happening right now!
Or Psalm 146:5-9 (again, my translation):

> Happy those whose help is Jacob's God,
> whose hope is in the Lord their God,

who is creating heaven and earth,
the seas and all that is in them,
keeping faith forever,
giving food to the hungry,
securing justice for the poor,
setting captives free.
The Lord is opening blind eyes
and straightening the bent,
raising up those who are bowed down,
comforting widows and orphans,
protecting the stranger,
loving the just,
but blocking the path of the wicked.
The Lord shall reign forever,
your God, Zion, through all generations!

Our God is a God of the living!

God's mighty deeds of creation and redemption are unending—they are going on right now! Therefore our praise must never stop. The reasons for giving praise to God are new every day. Every day we gather to sing God's praise. Today, every day, we will hear God's voice!

Shawn Carruth, OSB, has described this need to continually give praise in her reflection on the Liturgy of the Hours, especially the gospel canticles, the *Magnificat*, and the *Benedictus* (Luke 1:46-55, 68-79). Traditionally these canticles are sung every day at evening and morning praise. Carruth observes that this practice is similar to "women's work," or what we used to call "housework." You can never do the mega-laundry so that you don't have to do laundry again. You can never cook the mega-meal so that you don't have to cook ever again. In the same way, we are never finished with this praise of God. God is always ahead of us. God is always doing some wonderful work that has never been done before. We can never catch up. An insight worthy of Hallelujah![3]

The psalms teach us the rhythm of life: telling our story, crying out our pain, giving thanks, and praising God. As we pray the psalms frequently, we are becoming people of that rhythm, people who can enter into each moment of life. We are becoming people who can reflect on God's wonderful works in our lives and tell the story to others, people who can acknowledge our pain and anger honestly and turn over those feelings to God with complete candor and trust, people who can summon the whole world to give praise to our great and merciful God. We who pray the psalms regularly make a place for others to find that rhythm again of narrative, lament, and praise. It is, I think, our greatest ministry.

After more than fifty years of praying the psalms daily, I realize that Sister Lillian was right. The psalms do soak into one's bones. As John Cassian says:

> [We] will begin to repeat them and to treat them in [our] profound compunction of heart not as if they were composed by the prophet but as if they were [our] own utterances and [our] own prayer. . . . [We] will recognize that their words were not only achieved by and in the prophet in times past but that they are daily borne out and fulfilled in [us].
>
> For divine Scripture is clear and its inmost organs, so to speak, are revealed to us when our experience not only perceives but even anticipates its thought, and the meanings of the words are disclosed to us not by exegesis but by proof. . . . Thus we shall penetrate its meaning not through the written text but with experience leading the way.[4]

The psalms become a part of us. They teach us to be people who listen—to God, to Christ, to one another. They make us aware of all the wonders of creation—human and beast alike. They lead us to be people open to the future. And the final consequence of praying the psalms daily is the Psalter's first promise: "Happy will you be!" The first word of the Psalter is ʿashre, "happy." The Psalter begins with the promise that if we pray the psalms day and night we will be happy. Everything else leads back to the first promise: Praying the psalms daily will make us happy!

Our Sister Desideria was that happy person in the flesh. She lived to be 104, and led a typical monastic life. She did everything from working in the bakery to serving as assistant novice director. By the time she was ninety-five she was using a walker, and we all learned to keep our knees at a distance when we met her in the hall. She was so excited to see us that she would swing the walker energetically toward us. If you weren't doing a profound bow at her presence, you risked being clipped at the knees. But what she wanted to say to us was simply this: "It's all in the hymns!" She would repeat that phrase over and over to be sure we got it! By the time she reached one hundred, her refrain was "God loves you." The emphasis with which she announced this left no room for doubt. At 104 years of age she was simply smiling. She no longer needed words. She really was a hymn made flesh. These songs of praise soaked into her bones. So she leads us to the Psalter's last word: Hallelujah!

The Psalter ends with an incomplete hymn. Psalm 150 is all call to praise. The word that most characterizes that hymn and many others, "Hallelujah," is itself a call to praise. (Although we may think it's everywhere, it occurs only in last third of the Psalter, Tobit 13, and Revelation 19.) "Hallelu" is the plural imperative, "give praise." "Jah" is a form of the sacred name, "Yahweh." So hallelujah is a cry to everyone to praise the Lord! Every line of Psalm 150 begins with *hallelu* except the last one—which ends with *tehallel jah hallelu-jah!* That last line of the Psalter is the final call to praise: "Let everything that breathes praise the Lord! Praise the Lord [i.e., Hallelujah!]" (150:6). This cry to give praise is again a message for our lives. On January 9, 2002, Pope John Paul II said this about Psalm 150:

Although one might think that all created life should be a hymn of praise to the Creator, it is more correct to maintain that the human creature has the primary role in this chorus of praise. Through the human person, spokesman for all creation, all living things praise the Lord. Our breath of life that also presupposes self-knowledge, awareness and freedom (cf. *Prv* 20,27) becomes the song and prayer of the whole of life that vibrates in the universe. . . .

In union with the Son, perfect voice of the whole universe that he created, let us too become a constant prayer before God's throne.[5]

Psalm 150 is unfinished—it has only the call to praise but no reasons. Thus the Psalter itself is unfinished. We are left to finish the doxology, to give the reasons for praise, with our lives. Even through eternity we will not be finished with praise of our wonderful God. Praise is the goal of all prayer. All of our prayer reaches for Hallelujah!

Exercise:

1. Spend some time looking at and listening to the world around you. What are the things for which you want to praise God? *Remember: Hymns are about God more than they are about us.*

2. Think of the reasons in your personal life to praise God: individually and with those you love, for the past, the present, the future.

3. Think of all those who you want to call to help you give praise to God: the living, the dead, those not yet born. What created things do you want to join your song of praise? In nature (stars, rocks, birds, daisies, your pets), of human making (art, buildings, cooking, carpentry, knitting).

4. Decide which of these reasons and helpers you will use in your psalm. (You don't have to use them all. You can always write another hymn tomorrow!)

5. Gather all these together by the power of your memory to make present and write your hymn

- Begin with a call to praise.
- Give reasons for praise; use "for" or "because."
- Repeat this pattern at will (call and reasons).
- Possibly end with another call to praise. Hallelujah is a very good choice!

Postscript: My prayer for you, dear reader, is this: May the psalms enrich your life and your prayer. May you truly be "psalm-people." Please pray for me as well.

Suggested Psalm Classification by Genre

Laments			Hymns	
3	42–43	79	8	100
4	44	80	19:2-7	103
5	51	83	29	104
6	52	85	33	111
7	53	86	47	113
12	54	88	66:1-12	114
13	55	90	92	115
14	56	94	93	117
17	57	102	95	145
22	58	109	96	146
25	59	123	97	147
27:7-14	60	126	98	148
28	61	130	99	149
31	64	137		150
35	69	140		
36	70	141		
38	71	142		
39	74	143		
40:14-18	77			

Royal	Liturgies
2	15
20	24
21	26
45	50
72	67
89	68
101	81
110	82
144	132
	134

Thanksgiving	Confidence	Wisdom
9–10	11	1
18	16	19:7-15
30	23	37
32	27:1-6	49
34	62	73
40:1-13	63	112
41	91	119
65	108	127
66:13-20	121	128
75	125	133
107	131	139
116		
118		
120		
124		
129		
138		

Zion Songs	Historical
46	78
48	105
76	106
84	135
87	136
122	

Bibliography

Augustine. *Expositions of the Psalms.* Translated by Maria Boulding. 6 vols. Hyde Park, NY: New City Press, 2000–2004. A wonderful translation with insights into the christological interpretation of the psalms by an influential early Christian writer.

The Bible Documents: A Parish Resource. Chicago, IL: LTP, 2001. Contains all the important church documents on interpreting Scripture from *Divino Afflante Spiritu* (1943) to *The Interpretation of the Bible in the Church* (1993); also contains a commentary on each text. Very handy!

Davidson, Robert. *The Vitality of Worship: A Commentary on the Book of Psalms.* Grand Rapids, MI: Eerdmans, 1998. Very helpful exegesis of each psalm and its contemporary use.

Holladay, William L. *The Psalms through Three Thousand Years: Prayerbook of a Cloud of Witnesses.* Minneapolis: Fortress, 1993. A masterful study of the origins of the psalms and their use by Jews and Christians to the present.

John Paul II. *Psalms and Canticles: Meditations and Catechesis on the Psalms and Canticles of Morning Prayer.* Chicago, IL: LTP, 2004. From the pope's Wednesday audiences; inspiring meditations on all the psalms and canticles for Morning Prayer in the Roman Office.

Nowell, Irene. *Sing a New Song: The Psalms in the Sunday Lectionary.* Collegeville, MN: Liturgical Press, 1993. A meditative analysis of the Psalms in relation to the readings of each Sunday in the liturgical year.

Schaefer, Konrad. *Psalms.* Berit Olam. Collegeville, MN: Liturgical Press, 2001. Literary-critical approach to the psalms.

Wahl, Thomas Peter. *The Lord's Song in a Foreign Land: The Psalms as Prayer.* Collegeville, MN: Liturgical Press, 1998. Refreshing insights on the psalms in the Liturgy of the Hours.

Watson, Wilfred G. E. *Classical Hebrew Poetry: A Guide to Its Techniques.* Sheffield, England: Sheffield Academic Press, 1995. A bit technical, but everything you ever wanted to know about Hebrew poetry.

Notes

Chapter 1

1. Some of the material in this and subsequent chapters was originally published in *Tjurunga* (56 [May 1999]: 53–66) as "The Psalms: Living Water for Our Lives" and reprinted in *Benedictines* (52, no. 1 [Summer 1999]: 22–33). I am grateful for permission to include it here.

2. Demetrius Dumm, *Cherish Christ Above All* (Mahwah, NJ: Paulist, 1996; reprinted by St. Vincent's Archabbey, Latrobe, PA), 125.

3. John Paul II, "Psalms as Inspiration for Prayer" (March 28, 2001), reprinted in *Psalms and Canticles: Meditations and Catechesis on the Psalms and Canticles of Morning Prayer* (Chicago: Liturgy Training Publications, 2004), 9.

4. Translation from International Commission on English in the Liturgy (ICEL), *The Psalter* (Chicago, IL: LTP, 1994).

5. *RB 1980: The Rule of St. Benedict in Latin and English with Notes*, ed. Timothy Fry, et al. (Collegeville, MN: Liturgical Press, 1981). For more references to murmuring, see also RB 5.17–19; 23.1; 34.6; 35.13; 40.8–9; 41.5; 53.18.

6. Unless otherwise noted, all psalm translations are from Conception Abbey/The Grail, *The Revised Grail Psalms: A Liturgical Psalter* (Chicago, IL: GIA Publications, Inc., 2010).

7. Unless otherwise noted, all biblical translations (except for the Psalms) are from the *New Revised Standard Version*.

8. Bruno Barnhart, Monastic Forum at St. Meinrad, IN, January 11–12, 1998.

9. See Maria Boulding's masterful translation in *Expositions of the Psalms*, 6 vols. (Hyde Park, NY: New City Press, 2000–2004).

10. John Paul II, *Psalms and Canticles*, 8.

11. *Psalms: The Saint John's Bible*, handwritten and illuminated by Donald Jackson (Collegeville, MN: Liturgical Press, 2006).

12. Susannah Heschel in Doris Donnelly and John Pawlikowski, "Lovingly Observant," *America* (June 18–25, 2007): 12–13.

13. Demetrius Dumm, "The Biblical Foundations of Prayer," *American Benedictine Review* 24 (1973): 181–203.

14. My translation. The Hebrew *kilyot* (v. 7) means "kidneys." Both the Greek and the Latin Vulgate translate the word as "kidneys" (*nephroi* and *renes*, respectively). The kidneys were thought to be the seat of the conscience. The Hebrew root *kbd* (v. 9) means "heavy." The form that appears in the psalm (*kabod*, "glory") is usually emended to *kabed*, meaning "liver." (See Ludwig Koehler and Walter Baumgartner, *The Hebrew and Aramaic Lexicon of the Old Testament [HALOT]*, rev. by W. Baumgartner and J. J. Stamm, et al., trans. M. E. J. Richardson [New York: Brill, 2000], s.v. *kabed* II.) The liver, the heaviest organ of the body, was used as a term for "soul." The root meaning of the Hebrew *gil* (v. 9) is to dance or to turn around; it is often translated "rejoice" (*HALOT*, s.v. *gil*). In verse 9, the Greek Septuagint has "my tongue exults" (*egalliasato he glossa mou*). The Latin Vulgate has "my glory exults" (*exultavit gloria mea*) or "my tongue exults" (*exultavit lingua mea*). (St. Jerome made two translations, one from the Hebrew and one from the Greek.)

15. Paschal Botz, *Runways to God: The Psalms as Prayer* (Collegeville, MN: Liturgical Press, 1979), 1.

16. "Tenth Conference on Prayer," *John Cassian: The Conferences*, trans. Boniface Ramsey (Mahwah, NJ: Paulist, 1997), 10.11.5, 385.

Chapter 2

1. Michael Downey, "Understandings of God in a Changing Culture," in *Culture in Search of Spirituality: A Teleconference* (Notre Dame, IN: Retreats International, 1995).

2. Carol Christ, *Diving Deep and Surfacing: Women Writers on Spiritual Quest*, 2nd ed. (Boston: Beacon, 1980), 1. Christ is referring specifically to women's stories, and her point is painfully true that

they have not been told. But it is also true that many men's stories have not been told either. Telling our stories is essential for all of us.

3. Walter Brueggemann, *Theology of the Old Testament: Testimony, Dispute, Advocacy* (Minneapolis: Fortress, 1997), 134.

4. Ibid., 128.

5. Ibid., 145.

6. Walter Brueggemann, *The Prophetic Imagination*, 2nd ed. (Minneapolis: Fortress, 2001), 15–16.

7. Herbert Bronstein, ed., *A Passover Haggadah: The New Union Haggadah*, rev. ed. (New York: Central Conference of American Rabbis, 1974), 21; emphasis added.

8. ICEL, *The Roman Missal* (2010); emphasis added.

9. Brueggemann, *Theology*, 217.

Chapter 3

1. Demetrius Dumm, *Cherish Christ Above All* (Mahwah, NJ: Paulist, 1996; reprinted by St. Vincent's Archabbey, Latrobe, PA), 126–29.

2. Ibid., 124.

3. ICEL, *The Psalter* (Chicago, IL: LTP, 1994).

Chapter 4

1. See Mark Sheridan, "The Role and Interpretation of Scripture in the Rule of Benedict," *RB 1980*, 475.

2. John Cassian, *Institutes*, ed. Philip Schaff, Nicene and Post-Nicene Fathers, series 2, vol. 11 (Grand Rapids, MI: Eerdmans, 1894), 2.7.

3. Latin from Dom Louis Brou, ed. *The Psalter Collects* (London: Harrison and Sons, Ltd., 1949), 208; my translation.

4. Latin from ibid., 155; my translation.

5. Latin from ibid., 97–98; my translation.

6. Beth LaNeel Tanner, "Hearing the Cries Unspoken: An Intertextual-Feminist Reading of Psalm 109," *Wisdom and Psalms*, Feminist Companion to the Bible 2, ed. Athalya Brenner and Carole R. Fontaine (Sheffield: Sheffield Academic Press, 1998), 282–301.

7. Elizabeth Johnson, *Quest for the Living God: Mapping Frontiers in the Theology of God* (New York: Continuum, 2008), 66–67.

8. Leo Rosten, *The Joys of Yiddish* (Penguin Books, 1971), 4, quoted in Bruce Vawter, *Job and Jonah: Questioning the Hidden God* (New York: Paulist, 1983), 48.

Chapter 5

1. Beryl Schewe, "Thanksgiving for the Birth of a Child" (Psalm 116), Spring 2001.

2. Robert Davidson, *The Vitality of Worship: A Commentary on the Book of Psalms* (Grand Rapids, MI: Eerdmans, 1998), 379.

Chapter 6

1. Translation from *The Psalms: New American Bible 1991*, CCD (Collegeville, MN: Liturgical Press, 1991).

Chapter 7

1. See Konrad Schaefer, *Psalms*, Berit Olam: Studies in Hebrew Narrative and Poetry, ed.. David W. Cotter (Collegeville, MN: Liturgical Press, 2001), 66–67.

2. Saint Augustine, *Expositions of the Psalms*, trans. Maria Boulding, vol. 5 (Hyde Park, NY: New City Press, 2003), 525.

3. John W. Kiser, *The Monks of Tibhirine* (New York: St. Martin's Griffin, 2002).

4. Ibid., 192.

5. Ibid., 197.

6. Ibid., 244–45.

7. *RB 1980*.

Chapter 8

1. Augustine, *Expositions of the Psalms*, vol. 4, 424.

2. Thomas Peter Wahl, *The Lord's Song in a Foreign Land: The Psalms as Prayer* (Collegeville, MN; Liturgical Press, 1998), 138–39.

3. For a detailed analysis of the use of these three psalms in the Christmas liturgy, see Irene Nowell, *Sing a New Song: The Psalms in the Sunday Lectionary* (Collegeville, MN: Liturgical Press, 1993), 175–76, 178–79, 181–82.

4. *Adversus Haereses*, book 5, Preface.

Chapter 9

1. John Paul II, *Psalms and Canticles*, 9.

2. ICEL, *The Psalter* (Chicago, IL: LTP, 1994). I am using this translation here because of its crisp texture.

3. This image comes from a retreat conference given by Shawn Carruth in which she is quoting Peggy McIntosh, "Feeling Like a Fraud—Part III: Finding Authentic Ways of Coming into Conflict" (Paper No. WP90; 2000), 5–6. Carruth makes the connection to the Liturgy of the Hours.

4. Cassian, "Tenth Conference: On Prayer," 10.11.4–5, 384–85. Modified for inclusive language.

5. John Paul II, *Psalms and Canticles*, 94–95.

CPSIA information can be obtained
at www.ICGtesting.com
Printed in the USA
LVHW051321210221
679570LV00058B/2811